High Performance
Goal Setting

Dr. Beverly Potter

High Performance Goal Setting
Using Intuition to Conceive & Achieve Your Dreams
ISBN: 1-57951-012-4
Copyright © 2000 by Beverly A. Potter, Ph.D.

Published and Distributed by
RONIN Publishing, INc.
PO Box 522
Berkeley, CA 94701

Cover design by Judy July, Genertic type

Distributed to the trade by Publishers Group West

Printed in the United States of America
by Bertlesmann

9 8 7 6 5 4 3 2 1

Library of Congress Card Number: 00-190201

High Performance Goal Setting

Using Intuition To Conceive & Achieve Your Dreams

Dr. Beverly Potter

Ronin Publishing
roninpub.com

OTHER BOOKS BY DOCPOTTER

Overcoming Job Burnout
How to Renew Enthusiasm for Work

Finding a Path with a Heart
How to Go from Burnout to Bliss

Preventing Job Burnout
A Workbook

The Worrywart's Companion
Twenty-One Ways to Soothe Yourself
& Worry Smart

From Conflict to Cooperation
How to Mediate a Dispute

The Way of the Ronin
Riding the Waves of Change at Work

Drug Testing at Work
A Guide for Employers

Pass the Test
An Employee's Guide to Drug Testing

Brain Boosters
Foods & Drugs that Make You Smarter

The Healing Magic of Cannabis

Turning Around
Keys to Motivation and Productivity

Table of Contents

1. High Performance Goals	1
2. What is Intuition?	7
3. Becoming More Intuitive	16
4. Develop Your Intuitive Compass	26
5. Ask a Question	33
6. The Avoidance Trap	39
7. Powerful Goals	43
8. Use Magnetism	52
9. Mapping the Steps	59
10. Program Your Goals	64
11. Build Commitment	72
12. Acknowledge Progress	81
Recommended Reading	85
About Docpotter	87
Other Books by Docpotter	89

Chapter 1

High Performance Goals

There is an elementary difference, according to motivational experts, between highly successful people and others who go around in circles, getting nowhere. No, it is not gender, or race, or age, or education, or money, or even a happy childhood. The difference is that highly successful people use goals to get where they want to go.

People who use goals exude confidence, are action-minded, and expect to succeed. They tackle tough projects and have an eye for selecting activities where they are likely to succeed. They see their successes as a result of having created their own luck. People who set, pursue, and monitor career goals are more productive than people who simply work at a job. Basically, goal setters are confident, can-do people! Goals help you to get going—but you already knew that!

Resistance

Yet, there is something about setting goals that we resist. When asked about your goals, if you are like the rest of us, you shutter just a little as you suck in your stomach, set your jaw, and describe what you intend to achieve. There is something about setting goals and accomplishing them that is a regiment where, like a drill sergeant, you endeavor to squeeze more out of yourself. Too often it becomes a test of wills, where you fight a part of yourself that constantly undermines your best intentions.

Some people drive themselves, like steer to slaughter. Worst are perfectionists who set impossible standards, then whip themselves for not performing perfectly—all the time. We've all demanded too much of ourselves and know how it leads to procrastination and feeling guilty for not getting started. We backslide and avoid the very activities we must complete to move towards our dreams. No wonder a goal setting session can feel like a set up to fail.

Even worse, after all of this agony and effort, achieving the goal often doesn't bring the satisfaction we sought. How often have you discovered that you have made it to a place where you *don't want to be*—now that you've gotten there! It is a common career experience to spend years in training only to discover you don't like the work or that you feel like a misfit in the field of your expertise and find yourself wondering "what if" you had made different choices and followed a different path.

A Good Fit

Seeker: Why am I dissatisfied when I reach a goal I've worked hard to achieve?

Shaman Woman: Goals look beautiful when written out on paper, like a pair of fancy shoes in a store window.  You admire their style and dream of how wonderful it would be to wear those fancy shoes on your journey through life.

Seeker: But new shoes pinch my toes.

Shaman Woman: Yes, exactly! A shoe must be a good fit if it is to be of use. Fancy shoes that pinch your toes hobble you so you can hardly walk.

Seeker: What should I do?

Shaman Woman: Find shoes that fit you well, like the comfortable ones in the back of your closet. Wearing those shoes adds confidence to your journey which makes it easier to walk the trails and climb over the rocks.

Seeker: Do you mean that goals should fit like comfortable shoes?

Shaman Woman: Yes. When the goal is a good fit, it is molded to you—your values, your loves and dreams—then you easily achieve the steps to your goal, while having a joyous journey

Of course, you know setting goals is good for your career. But for a joyful journey, goals must be a good fit, resonating with your essential self. Unfortunately too often, the goals you set are a poor fit, pinching your spirit and hobbling you, as you force yourself onward.

I suspect you already know how to set and achieve goals. When you feel passionate about doing something, you do it, right? Of course you do! When motivated you can accomplish anything you set out to do. The problem most of us experience with goal setting is far deeper and broader. You need to step back and take a good look at how you select goals you pursue. It doesn't matter how swiftly a boat sails, if it is going in the wrong direction, it will end up at the wrong port.

Lopsided Thinking

When thinking of goals most people become very "practical" which engages rational-analytical mental capacities. We analyze, judge and systematize—all of which are essential once a goal has been conceptualized and we move into analysis to create an action plan for accomplishing it. The problem is that we usually neglect using intuition—our most useful capacity for uncovering goals that fit our values and dreams to provide a joyful journey.

Jane was a nurse for over fifteen years. She'd never really admitted, even to herself, that she was not happy in her work. Lately she'd been increasingly cranky—everything irritated her. On a lark, she accompanied her sister, also a nurse, to a psychic for a reading. The psychic immediately pegged her sister as a "healer" and went on and on about her healing abilities and what wonders she would accomplish in the future.

Dismissing it all as so much hokum, Jane expected a similar "trite" reading about her being a healer also. So she was startled when the psychic suddenly turned to her and said, "You've got your heart shielded because of so many people demanding nurturing from you. It's hardening you. You're in the wrong work. You should be working with horses."

This was amazing because she always loved horses and would like nothing better than to spend all her time at a stable. But long ago she had buried that dream. "It isn't practical," she told herself. "How can I make a living working with horses?" So instead she followed in her big sister's footsteps and went to nursing school because "there are always jobs for nurses!" That may be, but nursing was draining her. She gotten so she disliked her patients with their constant demands. Long ago she allowed analysis and logic to over-ride her intuition, which was telling her to follow horses.

The problem with traditional goal setting methodology is that it is lopsided, over emphasizing rational and logical processes, while neglecting the subjective and intuitive. This can lead to goals that look good on paper, that fit the bottomline, that impress family, friends, and your supervisor—but are a bad fit for you. You are not a robot to be programmed!

This lopsided thinking, thinking that relies solely on reason and neglects its sister, intuition, often yields goals that are a bad fit. A goal can look good to other people, but if it is a bad fit you run the risk of getting somewhere you didn't really  want to be. Worse, pursuing poorly fitting goals changes you. Eventually, you are molded to the misfitting goals you've achieved. These poorly fitting goals are now directing your life.

Hearing this makes some people nervous. They expect to be told in the next sentence to stop relying on reason and abandon sensible logic. These are valuable tools and we want to use them optimally—not indiscriminately and obsessively. Intuition and the subjective are tools as well—also valuable. Like a saw and a sander, each tool impacts wood in very different ways, each making its unique contribution. Try cutting through a board with sandpaper or smoothing a rough finish with a saw! Relying solely upon the skills of reason (logic, deduction, orderly sequences, judgment, and analysis) in goal setting is like doing just that!

High Performance Goal Setting

Most of us are expected to sustain continuous high level performance. And certainly goals are a time-honored tool for doing so. We have high performance brains, but don't engage them optimally when it comes to goal setting. We rely almost exclusively upon certain mental capabilities, while others lay dormant.

High performance goal setting employs all your mental capabilities, both rational-logical and intuitive-subjective in a yin/yang kind of balance and interplay. Learning how to use intuition can make dramatic changes in your life. Some people seem to be naturally able to extract and use intuitive information. They seem to reach conclusions, solve problems, sense reality quickly and easily in mysterious ways that others don't seem to be able to do. We generally see them as more intelligent, more creative and more sensitive.

Developing intuitive skills and applying them to goal setting will make a difference in your success, your happiness, your creativity and your decision making. In the following pages you will learn how to engage your quiet brain to create powerful goals—goals with such magnetism that they pull you towards them, so advancement takes less effort and you end up where you really want to be, while having a joyful journey.

Chapter 2

What is Intuition?

There is heated debate over what intuition actually "is". Some say it is a sixth sense, others insist it is the soul speaking, some believe it is a communication from the creator, or a guiding voice from one's guardian angel. For others it is an instinct, yet others describe intuition as a kind of high-speed computer-like processing of the millions of bits of data stored in our memory banks. While scientists and psychologists continue to wonder at the mystery of intuition, we know this for sure—it is universal and has been reported in every culture in the world throughout history. Everyone has experienced intuitive knowing, yet so little is understood about it.

Experts agree that intuition is a direct, and seemingly spontaneous, "knowing" about something but not knowing how you know. It is an "ah ha!"—an immediate comprehension about a situation that includes apprehensions, gut feelings, and inner knowledge. You "grok" it, which means to understand something so well that you simply "know" it. In Robert Heinlein's 1961 science fiction novel, *Stranger in a Stange Land*, grok is a Martian word meaning "to drink" and take it all in, to understand fully, or to be "at one with it". Intuition is a sudden insight, a process of tapping into a "wisdom" beyond the grasp of logic.

Intuition provides a gestalt—an understanding about the whole of the situation as compared to examining its parts, creating a kind of holographic knowing. The five senses bring in information about what is out there. "This is a leaf. It is green and grows on that tree. This is a bird. It has feathers." Intuitive knowing is an insight *about* the situation as a whole: "The tree and the bird depend upon one another. They are really one!"

Intuitive knowing comes as a spark or a trace of an idea rather than as a fully realized concept. Information bubbles up from the inside. Intuition speaks to us through images and symbols, through feelings and emotions and through physical sensations. Its messages are fleeting and subtle, more easily heard when the mind and body are calm.

Intuition often contradicts physical facts with a feeling that a certain circumstance is not what it appears to be. We've all had the experience of "sensing" that a transaction will lead to trouble even though all indicators suggest otherwise, for example. Listening to intuition is an act of faith—faith in your own wisdom. "I know what I know!" Phrases like "My gut tells me", "It feels right", "A light bulb went off" all indicate an intuitive process.

Behind the Scenes Thinking

The brain is constantly busy chewing over problems behind the scenes, so to speak. The latest research suggests that there are mechanisms that enable the brain to soak up and ruminate on information, looking for subtle patterns and connections, behind your back—without the aid of words, and in most cases without your even being conscious of what's going on. Additionally, latest research points to the brain having two memory systems—one for explicit memories that we can recall and one for implicit memories outside of conscious awareness. The result is a body of useful, experienced-based knowledge that steers you through everyday life—knowledge you are unconscious of ever acquiring and cannot express in words.

Intuitive Thinking

Reasoning works with details, data, facts and bits of information. It uses deductive rules to examine, order and shape data into conclusions and judgments. We trust our rationalizations because we have logical rules we can follow step-by-step to hold on to. If A and B, then C. We can see each step in a logical progression. It seems very real—very "right".

Intuition is another kind of mental process that is different from rational thought, but equally important. When you "figure things out" for yourself, you're using intuitive reasoning to discover general principles about a situation. Intuition feels like a spontaneous understanding about something. It may not come immediately, however. In fact, more often it comes after you've gathered and digested a great deal of facts about the concern at hand. Whether intuition is actually "spontaneous" or not, we don't know because little is understood about how it works or where it occurs—physiologically.

Intuition is a nonlinear, nonempirical process of gaining and interpreting information. Nonlinear means it does not proceed in logical steps. It is interesting to note that most descriptions of intuitive processes are framed in terms of its being "*non*" reason—*non*linear, *non*empirical, *ir*rational, *un*conscious—revealing again our romance with reason. More importantly, it shows we are literally at a loss for words when it comes to intuition. We know more about what intuition "is not" than we understand what intuition "is".

Implicit Learning

It is no longer thought that intuition happens in one place in the brain, and that logical thought happens somewhere else—the old right brain/left brain theory. Intuition and logical thought are different *modes* of brain functioning. Most neuropsychologists agree that when you learn to ride a bike or play the piano, for example, your brain lays down memories about muscle coordination and timing that can't be expressed in words, but are part of your learning nonetheless. Whether other types of knowledge are stored "implicitly" in the brain has been hotly debated for more than thirty years.

The latest research suggests that intuitive insights are the result of spreading networks of electrical activation in the brain. Over time, more associations are drawn in, allowing less effective approaches to dissolve and other possible solutions to present themselves.

Thinking about a problem, like how to design a flier, how to solve a programming glitch, or solving a puzzle, for instance, stimulates hot spots of electrical activity in areas of the brain's cortex dealing with the particular area of knowledge. It starts off small and focused but gradually ripples out through the brain, broadening the network of possible solutions. How this happens is a mystery. What is known is that words and rational thinking get in the way of the brain's silent problem solving. One explanation is that verbal reasoning impedes the "spreading activation" because it engages the prefrontal cortex, a part of the brain that can close down electrical activity elsewhere.

Intuition and Goal Setting

The human brain is often been compared to an iceberg where about 7% is visible above the ocean's surface—which parallels how much of the brain most people use—93% lies hidden below the surface. Intuition taps into that mysterious 93% of your mind's capability lying silently below the surface.

When you use your intuitive capabilities together with your rational mind you use more of your mind's capacity. Another metaphor for using intuition along with reason is that it is like using both hands to accomplish something, rather than just one. Thinking of the relationship between intuition and reason is like the ying and the yang, which are opposites, yet they work together to balance and compliment one another. Reason draws from the details and the individual facts, while intuition draws from the overview and subjective generalizations.

Gathering and processing information is central to goal setting. We gather facts and information, which are assembled and weighted according to various rules of logic. We also gather information in intuitive ways. Intuition gathers information from physical sensations, impressions and symbols. Our senses bring in an enormous amount of input that never reaches conscious awareness but is weighed mysteriously, "behind the scenes". It's hard to discuss because intuition goes on without words and we use words to communicate thoughts. It's a kind of paradox. Fortunately, you don't have to solve the paradox to benefit from its power.

Business Tool

An obscure meaning for "intuit" is to tutor, to instruct. When you are in tune with your intuition and you stop to listen to it, it does just that. Intuition provides instruction. Intuition is an internal guidance system, your personal wisdom drawing upon associations and memory, past experience and something unknown.

Successful business people think of intuition as an ally, because they realize that the rational mind doesn't necessarily give the best answers. A study of business executives worldwide, sponsored by the International Management Institute in Geneva, Switzerland, showed that fifty-four percent used intuition in business about equally with logic, while thirty percent of the successful business people studied said they used intuition even more than logic and reason in their personal lives.

Amorphous and ill defined, as it is, intuition has to be nurtured and trusted to turn it into a powerful goal setting tool. Intuition speaks in a different language. It is symbolic and fragmentary. Many intuitive flashes can pass you by when you are not trained to notice them. It often doesn't make sense at first, so it is easy to dismiss it. You need to attune yourself to the language of intuition to reap its benefits. When you know what you are reacting to and why, you can make clearer decisions and set more powerful goals.

Wisdom and Business Savvy

Intuition is a kind of natural wisdom. It provides understanding about situations, especially when there's limited hard information. In business—and life, for that matter—we never have all the information we need all the time. Each situation is different and there is a delicate balance between being indecisive and impulsive. If you hold off making a decision until every last fact is in and your success is guaranteed, the opportune time to act will certainly have past. If, on the other hand, you take bold goals and act on too little information, you are rash and impulsive. This is  where intuition is a loyal ally if you listen and trust it. When it comes to deciding when to act quickly and when to hold back in reserve, your intuition will help you to determine what action to take and when to take it.

Obstacles to Intuition

While we all have innate intuitive ability, many people are deaf to it much of the time. Sometimes we discount this precious wisdom or don't even hear it at all. There are a number of things that can muffle your intuition.

Jumping to Conclusions

Jumping to conclusions is a rush to judgement—once made your mind is closed. Drawing conclusions and making judgements are one in the same process. It is a rational-logical process and shuts down intuition. We all know that conclusions often are wrong!

Expert Mind

Experts know everything. When you approach situations with an "I know" attitude your mind is closed to the possibility that there is something about the situation that you don't know. You don't pay attention because you stop looking; you don't hear because you stopped listening. You miss and dismiss anything that doesn't fit your "expert" opinion. You stop learning and you probably don't know it.

A Cup of Tea

Seeker: I'm really interested in intuition. Would you teach me what you know? Don't you think intuition is . . . .

Shaman Woman: [Interrupting] Would you like some tea?

The Shaman carefully filled the Seeker's cup until it was full. She paused for a moment, then began pouring again as the cup overflowed.

Seeker: Yes, thanks. I think intuition is . . . . Ack! What are you doing? Stop! No more will go in—the cup is overflowing!

Shaman Woman: Like the cup, you are so filled with your ideas about intuition that nothing else can go in.

Practice Having a Beginner's Mind

To avoid the expert mind and jumping to conclusions, you must hold back and remain suspended in uncertainty rather than racing to premature closure. You can do this by practicing a beginner's mind. Approach things as if you are doing them for the first time—like a beginner. It pulls you into the present moment, the here-and-now. You become more attentive and life takes on freshness.

Desire

Desire has two faces. It can help or inhibit intuition. Helpful desire directs your energy to focus on something positive you want to move towards. Other times desire gets into the way when you are too attached to something. This attachment overrides and silences intuition. You don't hear, see or know anything that conflicts with your desire. Desire can trick you with very clever arguments, which turn off intuition and run over common sense to satisfy itself, as we see in addictions, compulsions and fixations.

Fear

Fear is a major obstacle to intuition because it stops you from trusting your inner wisdom. Don't try to abolish fear because it is your friend. Instead, treat it as an ally.

There is good fear and problem fear. Good fear warns of danger. This kind of fear is very akin to intuition and could be thought of as intuitive fear. It is a knowing and is generally neutral, without emotion. Problem fear, on the other hand, is associated with anxiety and trepidation, even panic.

Intuition does not reason, it simply "knows". Not knowing how you know something is worrisome because our formal education teaches us to use the rules of logic to examine available information to draw conclusions. Not knowing how you know something can, itself, create anxiety. You have no basis, nothing to hold on to.

You're skeptical, and demand verification and logical explanations. This anxiety and grabbing for explanations, shuts down, overruns, drowns out, and smothers intuition. It's a paradox like sex, where you have to "let go", because judging performance turns off the sexual energy. Intuition is similar. As soon as reason kicks in, intuition is muffled and silenced.

Problem fear messages are usually accompanied by strong feelings of anxiety whereas intuitive fear messages warning of danger are neutral, without the element of anxiety—you simply know a threat is near. Problem fear is debilitating. It paralyzes and inhibits progress toward goals or stops it altogether, while intuitive fear is an ally guiding you around obstacles.

Chapter 3

Becoming More Intuitive

You are already intuitive. We all are. You use your intuition all time; but since you probably haven't learned to recognize it, you don't realize how often you actually call on it. Intuition tends to be ephemeral and transparent, so elusive that it is easily ignored. Intuition emerges first as a formless impression. When your circuits are jammed with worry, road rage, and daily mental chatter, you can't hear intuition's subtle messages. As you learn to listen more deeply you discover answers to pressing concerns. The more you cultivate intuition the more you can make use of the synchronicity all around you.

Cultivate Your Ability

Trusting your natural intuitive ability gets easier as you exercise it. It is a little like learning to ride a bike. Balancing on two wheels is not something that can be forced. Trying harder gets in the way rather than helping. It is "easy" and "effortless" once you "get it", but getting it takes a kind of "letting go" which feels as if you might fall over, making you freeze up again.

When you were learning to ride a bike you already knew a lot about balance because you can walk on two legs. Your learning to ride a two-wheeler drew upon your intuitive understanding of balance, which you acquired when learning to walk. At first you were tight as you tried to forcibly control the bike, but when you relaxed, let go and tuned into your intuitive understanding of balance, your body sudden "got it"! And just as suddenly you could ride a two-wheeler.

Your sprouting intuitive ability grows faster and more robust when it is facilitated with fertile soil. A playful attitude rooted in a firm base of knowledge, maintaining a quiet mind, thinking with symbols rather than words, paying attention to surroundings, and tuning into feelings are conditions that nurture intuition's growth, especially when first experimenting with it.

Build a Foundation of Knowledge

Intuition doesn't work on a blank slate. If you're a social worker, the likelihood of getting insights about the intricacies of the theory of relativity are pretty slim. Intuition operates best in areas you have a passion for, where you are schooled, and have a lot of practical experience. The greater your knowledge in the topic of concern the easier it will be for you to tap into intuition with regards to it.

Breathe Slowly and Deeply

Smooth, slow, deep breathing facilitates receiving intuitive guidance. This is probably the reason that most spiritual practices encourage deep breathing during prayer and mediation.

Many people hold their breath or breath shallowly, especially in stressful situations which shuts them off from their intuitive guidance. When you catch yourself doing this, stop and deliberately breathe slowly and deeply from your diaphragm. Breathe in slowly through your nostrils, filling your lungs and then slowly empty your lungs by pushing the air out your mouth. Make the in breaths the same length as the out breaths. Think of breathing in and out as one continuous smooth loop. Quietly notice thoughts, ideas and hunches that come. Notice feelings and images. Notice what you know.

Ask a Question

Intuition works best when directed towards a question. When you sit silently and focus on a particular concern stated as a question, images will come to mind, seemingly of their own accord. We've all had this experience.

You can ask your question aloud, silently in your mind, write it down, or type it into your computer. "What is it that I really love doing?" or "If I won the lottery and didn't have to work, what would I do?" or "If I go into hair dressing how will I feel about touching people?" are examples.

Sit quietly; still your mind. Wait patiently and notice hunches, thoughts and ideas that come into your mind. This is intuition in action.

Let Go

When you have an important decision about a goal you are wise to school yourself in all the issues pertaining

to it by gathering information from many sources. When you feel sufficiently confident in your knowledge of the issues, then ask your intuition a question, such as how to transform a difficult situation into a beneficial one. Then set it aside. Take a break. Do something else entirely. Go to a movie. Visit with a friend. Take a walk. Pay the bills. Refocus your mind onto something else.

After a prolonged endeavor of intensive thought, new ideas will begin to surface when you take a break from the activity. Intuition will work away behind the scene solving your dilemma in some mysterious, silent way. The essence of letting go is releasing expectations and setting aside the urge to do something. Just let things unfold. Don't try to force an answer.

Maintain a Playful Attitude

Sometimes it can be a while before an image or feeling appears to you. This is normal. It is important not to "try". You can prime the pump, so to speak, by "pretending" much the way you did as a child. Just make it up. Ask yourself, "If I did have an intuition about this issue it would be . . ." Or, "If I had to make a decision now it would be . . ." Or just make up a story about what is going to happen relative to your inquiry.

"Am I pretending?", you may ask. Answer is yes; you are making it up. Where do these impressions come from if not from you? It is your imagination, your mind, and your intuition that produces intuitive knowing. Just because you feel that you are making it up does not mean, however, that the impressions are invalid—they are valid for you because they come from you.

An important step in developing intuitive awareness is learning to accept your sensory knowing. Your ability to pretend is an important part of the intuitive learning process. Don't worry if it doesn't make immediate sense.

Use pretending as a way to experiment with knowing. Imagine that everything has meaning and look for applications of that meaning.

Pretending is a valuable ability when learning new skills. It helps to pretend that we have already acquired the skills. "Act as if"—"Fake it and you'll make it".

Actually, much of math and scientific progress has been built upon pretending—make believe. It is called the "hypothesis". A hypothesis is a "let's suppose this is true" kind of statement which scientists and mathematicians then try to refute. The hypothesis, this pretending, is a powerful tool in making discoveries and shaping reality.

Quiet Your Mind

A door to your intuitive self opens when you quiet your mind of outside stimulation and mental chatter. The rational mind is almost never silent, but dominates consciousness most of the time with "mental chatter". Yet, there is a second "mind"—the quiet mind that is always turned on and attentive. Your ability to tap into your personal wisdom is determined largely by the quality of your quiet mind skills.

Some people get their best ideas while walking in the woods, soaking in a bubble bath, when they let their minds go adrift. Intuitive processes improve as you experiment with quieting your mind. Creative breakthroughs often occur when the mind is in a semi-con-scious dream-like state just before entering REM sleep, for example.

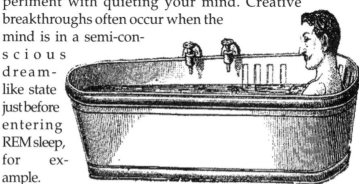

Daydream

Imagination, like pretending, is a medium for intuition. The more you exercise your imagination, the better you get at using it to channel your intuitive knowing. The power of your imagination is unlimited when it comes to answering questions, solving problems and reaching goals.

Actively visualize possible solutions to problems. Have pencil and paper to write down ideas as they come. Ideas may pop into your head at other times, while driving car or washing dishes, for example. Daydream. Visualize situations and outcomes. Play out scenarios in your head. Imagine what life will be like when you have attained your goal. Picture the benefits and rewards? Dream up novel ways of achieving your goal.

Pay Attention

There are infinite things in world to catch your attention. What you notice is not coincidence; meaning is attached to it. There is nothing in life that doesn't have meaning. Every moment, past, present and future has a meaning. Every sign, every act, every deed, everything we notice has significance.

Mostly we don't pay attention to what we notice or how we choose to notice some things and not other things. This is done somehow by our subconscious, which collects and coalesces what we notice into meaningful patterns. In fact, we go around a lot of time actively ignoring what we notice. But you can stop and actually notice what you notice—pay attention to what you are noticing and the way in which you are noticing it because you are actually making decisions about what to notice. The simple act of paying attention has great power.

Try this experiment. Look around the room and notice everything that is red. Really pay attention to red things. Now, close your eyes and picture the space around you and notice the red things in it. Good. That was pretty easy, right?

Now, close your eyes again. Again picture the space around you and this time notice all the brown things in it. Then open your eyes and look around. You probably see many brown things you didn't see in your mental picture. You weren't paying attention to brown things before, now you are.

Practice a broad attentiveness. Tune into the whole environment—both internal and external—including the sounds, sensations, physical feelings, textures, light, ideas, hunches, images symbols, and so forth. Notice subtleties, and changes. Make comparisons. Broad attentiveness is opposite of the pointed attention to details you use when making bookkeeping entries, for example.

Notice the choices that you make. Notice what you notice. You may discover that you notice mostly negative things, for example. A way to lead yourself is to decide what you will notice and then practice noticing it until it becomes habitual. By deliberately noticing something, you set the direction you are moving in a way that becomes self-perpetuating, yet feels natural and effortless.

You can develop a pull towards a goal by deliberately noticing positive, attractive aspects of it. You can look at images representing your goal's positive qualities and allow the images to speak to you. Use metaphors to tell the story of where you want to go or what you want to achieve.

Notice Symbols

Images are the natural language of the quiet mind, which speaks without words. Intuition is not literal, but speaks through the language of symbols. Intuitive knowing comes as pictures and impressions, proceeding irregularly by associative links rather than by logical steps.

When solving a problem, avoid words and don't try too hard. Research shows that the brain handles verbal and nonverbal knowledge in different ways and doesn't do a good job of mixing the two. Verbalization impairs intuitive sensitivity. If you want to get the most from your intuitive mind, don't strive to put into words pieces of knowledge that are essentially nonverbal—the look of a face or of a color, because it disrupts the flow of intuitive, nonverbal thought.

Set aside step-by-step logic and scientific methodology. Instead, call up associations, opposites, and metaphors. Turn ideas around. Pose ridiculous questions. Suppose the opposite. Ask, "What if?".

Tune into Physical Sensations

Sensations are messages. Your body is telling you something. Your body is smart. Are you listening? People use the word "gut" to describe instinctive intuition because information registers in the belly. Scan your body for sensations. What do you feel and where do you feel it?

Personal Intuitive Style

We tend to be the most intuitive about the things we engage in daily, especially when it is something important, having to do with our families, careers and hobbies.

The intuitive information you receive is always valid just the way physical sensations are "valid" even though you may not know what they mean. If you have an ache in your back you may not know what caused it or how to get rid of it. But it is real. Intuitive knowing is similar. You may not know where it came from or what it means. But you "know". Maybe you have "a funny feeling" about a situation, for example. Sometimes people are out of touch with intuition because they expect it to be absolutely literal and they discount anything that is not.

Discover Your Symbols

The same symbol can have different meanings for different people and different meanings for one person in different situations. We build up a unique symbolic vocabulary as we make our way through life. For example, you may have had a birdhouse outside your window as a child. Seeing a bird or birdhouse will have a unique meaning for you. If the image of a birdhouse comes to mind when thinking about a problem, for example, it is probably telling you something about the situation at hand. One of the first steps is to identify your unique symbolic language. As you work with it you'll find that you actually do have an intuitive vocabulary that is consistent and reliable in its meaning.

Uncover Your Style

Intuition is unique and personal. We each have our own intuitive language. Intuition comes from within you through a symbol, or an image, or a sensation, or a voice. Only you can interpret your signals. It can feel like you are talking to yourself, especially when intuition is auditory. And, of course, you are! You are tapping into your deeper wisdom.

Getting a sense of your unique intuitive style builds confidence. What type of information do you get? Become familiar with how you communicate with your intuition. Intuition can come through a seeing mode, a sensing mode, or a hearing mode. It comes in fragmentary images, feelings and voices. It takes practice to assemble the bits and pieces into something that makes sense.

Intuition is always individualized. Developing your intuitive style involves getting to know how intuition feels to you and identifying your way of getting information. When you know your intuitive method, confidence to use it grows.

Exercises can speed up your development. There are numerous books filled with helpful techniques for cultivating intuition. I've included a list of recommended reading at the end of this book. I especially like the work of Laura Day, whose books are filled with fascinating exercises.

You'll find that you have certain preferences, rituals or techniques that are more conducive to calling out your intuition than others. Do you work better in the morning or at what time of day? Do you like your eyes open or closed? Do you prefer to write your question down or read it out loud?

Images and impression themselves are not intuition, however, they are the medium of intuition, like oils are a painter's medium. Just like words are not thought, but they are the medium of thinking. Images and impressions bring intuitive knowing into the conscious.

You learn your style by observing it. When experiencing an intuitive feeling, image or sensation just notice it—without analysis. Writing down your observations in a journal is helpful. Describe your experience. After you've noted many such observations, read them over, looking for patterns will help you discover your intuitive style. As you do this you will develop a deeper trust of your feelings, hunches, visions and sensations.

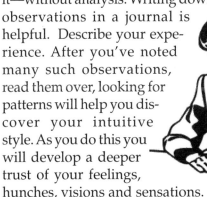

Chapter 4

Develop Your Intuitive Compass

Goals help us to achieve something or to get somewhere. You may be seeking advancement in your work, or striving for personal development. Your goals may have to do with relationships, or with money.

Goals are a tool for getting from here to somewhere else in the future. At the time that you set the goal, the outcome you seek is still an idea, an envisioning, a dream. To achieve your objective, manifest your vision, or make your dream come true, you must forge a path from here and now to the accomplishment of your goal in the future.

It is easy to get lost. Traditionally, people find their way through the wilderness by using a compass and reading the stars. A compass is a tool that enables you to get your bearing. It tells you where you are relative to a certain point, like the North Pole. Similarly, an Intuitive Compass helps you get your internal bearings so you can stay on course to achieving your goals. Without a compass you can be working diligently, but still go around and around, even backwards, without realizing it. Without a firm fix on your bearings you can reach a goal only to find that it is not where you really wanted to go, because the objective itself was in the wrong direction! When you have a compass you can be surer of your direction which builds confidence to venture further.

Because pictures and metaphors engage intuition, the tools explored in this book are presented metaphorically to enable you to use them to communicate with your intuition. Your intuition understands the pictures that meaningful metaphors call up.

Intutitive Compass

A compass is a navigational tool with a needle that reliably points to North because of the magnetic qualities of the earth. As you will discover later in this book powerful goals use principles of magnetism as well.

To use a compass, you line the needle pointing north up with the "N" marker on the compass face. Then, when you stand facing North, you know east is to your right, west to your left, and south is behind you. You can now proceed west, with confidence, for example, stopping periodically to check your compass and correct your course.

Metaphorically your Intuitive Compass works the same way, only "North" is an internal state.

Calibrating Your Compass

Before you can use your Intuitive Compass you must calibrate it. Using experiences—blissful and burnout moments—as North and South poles accomplish this.

The earth's poles exert magnetism, which expresses itself as either an attractive pull or a repulsive push. Similarly the needle on your Intuitive Compass is pulled towards bliss or repulsed by burnout.

How to Calibrate

Begin the calibration process by creating a reference point anchored to this moment, right here and now. Imagine having an Objective Eye, which observes, dispassionately without judging. Stop reading and for a few seconds allow your Objective Eye to notice how you feel right now. Notice your physical well-being. Notice sensations in your body. With your Eye, notice your emotional state, you're spiritual state.

How do you feel right now? Use a scale from 1 to 10 to rate your well-being. Let 1 be poor and a very low sense of well-being and let 10 be optimal and a very high sense of well-being. Rate your well-being at this moment and write the rating in your journal or on the corner of this page. In the scientific world, this rating is called a "baseline", which is an anchor, a point of reference, a starting point, a point of comparison.

Calibrating Repulsion

The burnout pole of your Internal Compass is established first. Begin by identifying a burnout situation from your past. For our purposes here, burnout situations are those where you felt used up, consumed, dissipated, and sapped. It will probably be a work situation because they seem to be the easiest to remember. It might be an event in an otherwise positive situation or a point in time, an interaction or situation where you felt you were burning out.

It doesn't have to be the worst situation in your life. In fact, don't use "heavy" situations for practice because the feelings can be so strong that they can overpower you. Instead, pick a mild to moderately difficult situation that you thought of at the time as a burnout. Write down a description of the burnout situation in your journal.

For about a minute bring the burnout time back into your mind, making it as real as you can. Call on your Objective Eye, which doesn't judge but simply sees, to notice how the burnout situation feels. Notice what you were thinking at the time. Notice physical sensations you had. Notice your level of well-being. Notice what made the situation a burnout. Do this now. Put the book down and take a few seconds to re-experience the burnout situation.

Before doing anything else, bring out your well-being scale again. With 1 being very poor well-being and 10 being optimal well-being, rate your well-being at this moment and write your rating down in your journal.

How did you feel after reliving the burnout situation? If you are like most of us, your well-being rating was lower than the baseline rating that you made before starting this exercise. Your Objective Eye probably noticed a downer, depressed feeling. It may have been subtle; or it may have been strong. Your Eye probably observed more negativity in your thinking—more pessimism, more punitiveness, and more judgmental thinking that provokes guilt and anxiety. Spiritually, your Eye may have noticed more desperation, less hope and a loss of faith. Right now, you probably feel a little down. Your energy, your enthusiasm, your spark has been diminished—burned out—just a little.

To calibrate the repulsive force of your Compass, you must become very familiar with these feelings, thoughts, and sensations. Let your Eye study them. The more finely-tuned your Compass, the more sensitive you will be to signs of potential burnout in situations so you can avoid them or prepare to meet him.

Chances are that as your Eye watched the burnout situation you observed feeling of powerlessness, helplessness, and loss of control. It may have been a damned-if-you-do, damned-if-you-don't situation where you were disempowered, for example.

Allow your Objective Eye to compare your sensations of well-being at the baseline—your first anchor—with those you experienced when reliving the burnout situation.

Use this comparison as a reference point. You can think of it as a kind of handle or toehold. Can you see how you are using rational-logical thinking devices to reach into and get a hold on a portion of your quiet mind that is difficult to think about?

It is through this kind of process that you can get more control over your psyche which operates unconsciously. The greater your access to such seemingly ethereal aspects of your mental functioning, the greater your capability for performing at a consistently high level.

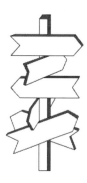

Which Path Shall I Take?

Seeker: I have so many options. Which path should I pursue?
Shaman Woman: Where do you want to go?
Seeker: Hummm, I'm not really sure.
Shaman Woman: Then any path will take you there.

Calibrating Attraction

The attractive force of your Compass is explored and established in the same manner, this time by reliving and observing blissful moments. A blissful moment is a time when you were so involved in what you were doing that you "forgot" about yourself. In a sense, you merged into the moment. It is a time when what you were doing was working—when everything came together serendipitously. This blissful moment is characterized by a sense of time standing still. You feel in control of the situation without trying to control it. Creative ideas come to you spontaneously, without thinking. You feel empowered, enthusiastic and being "one with" what you are doing.

You may have experienced blissful moments while playing sports. When playing tennis, for example, the racket becomes an extension of your arm. You don't

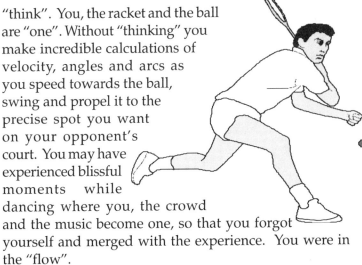

"think". You, the racket and the ball are "one". Without "thinking" you make incredible calculations of velocity, angles and arcs as you speed towards the ball, swing and propel it to the precise spot you want on your opponent's court. You may have experienced blissful moments while dancing where you, the crowd and the music become one, so that you forgot yourself and merged with the experience. You were in the "flow".

To calibrate the attractive pole on your Compass, recall a blissful moment. It may have been this morning, last week, last year or a long time ago. As before, relax and project yourself back into the experience: relive it, making it as vivid as you can. As you do, allow your Eye to notice how the blissful moment feels. What are the sensations? What thoughts were in your mind? Without judging, let your Eye notice what happened and observe the big picture of the experience. Make sure to notice what made the moment blissful. Put the book aside and recall a blissful moment for a few seconds.

Good! Again, rate your well-being on a scale from 1 to 10, with 1 being very low on well-being and 10 being very high. Stop reading now and allow your Eye to rate your well-being at this moment. Write the rating in your journal.

If you are the rest of us, your well-being went up after recalling the blissful moment. You probably feel more empowered and more enthusiastic. You probably have more stamina, yet are more relaxed. You probably have a sense of greater faith and more hope about the future. These kinds of pleasurable feelings comprise the attractive pole of your Intuitive Compass.

Fine-Tuning

Repeat this exercise often with several different burn-out and blissful situations until you can recognize the attraction of bliss and the repulsion of burnout right away. The idea is to really get a feeling, a strong sense, an indescribable recognition of these inner states. As you do you open a channel to receiving information from your intuition.

When you come to a fork in the road, stop to read your Compass to determine which path to follow. Check the direction your goals are taking you. Are they magnetic and pulling you, or repulsive and pushing you?

Chapter 5

Ask a Question

Your life is a mosaic of all your decisions to this point, combining to form a picture of who you are. Past decisions have a momentum that keep you going in the same direction, so that your future is shaped by your past. Past decisions make you who you are today. While past decisions can dictate your future, your current decisions can set you free because you chart the course of your life with your day-by-day decisions.

Each waking moment you are making decisions, from what to wear and what to eat for breakfast, to how to invest your money, and who to marry. Behind each goal is a decision; behind each decision is a question.

Life is continually seeking answers. Everything we do consists of answering questions. Actually, most of the time we are not conscious of many of the questions we ask. When driving, for example, you may wonder "Is that driver going to pull in front of me?" Questions such as these flash through your mind almost constantly.

The trick is to become more skilled at bringing intuitive knowing into consciousness where you can use it even more effectively. You tap into your intuition by listening. The easiest way to initiate communicate with your intuition is by asking questions.

Call on your intuition when making decisions, even little ones like deciding what to eat for breakfast. Restate the decision as a question. "Shall I eat eggs for breakfast today?" Then wait and listen. Use your Intuitive Eye to notice how your body responds. "Shall I eat cereal?" Notice again. Opportunities to practice abound everyday, no matter what you are doing. Ask questions about which route to take to work, which phone call to answer and which to let go to voice mail.

As you practice you become aware of the numerous choice points you pass through each day and the questions you have been asking but were unaware of doing so. In the same way, you can listen for answers from your intuition about larger questions.

Engage Intuition

Questions organize where you direct your attention. Questions are a portal to intuition. Questions focus intuition and tell your quiet mind what to notice in the world around you. The intuitive state is receptive—a state of waiting, letting go of expectations. Using intuition is a matter of focusing, asking and peacefully listening without effort or strain. Notice what comes to mind and what things draw your attention. Intuitive information is received in response to a question. There are two steps. First answers come in symbols; next you must make meaning out of the information received.

Ask a Question

Ask a question in a peaceful environment, such as when relaxing in bed or when taking a leisurely walk away from the hustle and bustle. Then wait and listen to the thoughts that float to the surface. Allow one impression to suggest another, going from one association link to another. Be careful not to force the answer you "should" get because there are no "right" answers.

An answer may not come immediately. Sometimes you might have to approach a question from different angles by rephrasing it. It may even take several days of asking your question before an answer manifests in your daily activities. Answers usually come symbolically and may not be recognized as an "answer". Being aware and trusting that an answer will come is key to opening intuition.

Clues can come to mind as metaphors, images, or even in a dream. The answer, in a sense, drops into your mind. When intuitive knowing comes it is detached, without emotion. When impressions are accompanied by strong feelings of fear or other emotions, they are probably anxiety or worry, not an intuition. The same is true of messages telling you what you "should" do.

Techniques for Receiving Intuitive Answers

You can develop your intuition like any other skill. It just takes practice. Having a structure for receiving intuitive information makes it easier to recognize, just as thinking is improved with the structure and rules of logic.

When faced with a problem, choice or decision write it down. Relax and then restate your dilemma as a question and write it next to the first statement. Hold the question in your mind with a high degree of concentration and simply listen to what reverberates, like ripples when a stone is dropped into a still pool.

Following are several popular techniques for receiving intuitive answers. They are fun and you can put them to the test of science by keeping a record your experiences in your journal. Later you can go back and rate the quality of your decisions and to what degree the answers helped.

The Traffic Signal

Imagining a traffic light can help give your intuition a voice about situations. After asking your question, let go of what you hope the answer will be. Instead, allow an image of a traffic signal with red, yellow and green lights to come to mind. If you're good at envisioning, you might imagine walking or riding along a street with a traffic light a short way ahead. As you approach notice what color is shining—red, yellow or green. Even if you don't "see" the signal, imagine what color would be shining if you could see it. Red means "Stop!" yellow means "Wait" or "Go slowly"; green means "Go".

This is a wonderful technique because you can take it anywhere. When faced with a choice where you must make a quick decision quickly check the traffic light. Try it for a week or two and see how it works for you.

Flip a Coin

This technique is so old it seems almost trite to mention it. Relax and concentrate on your question. Then flip a coin and notice how you *hope* the coin will fall. This anticipatory feeling is often an intuitive message.

Use a Pendulum

A pendulum is a weighted object on a string or a neck chain that can swing freely. A ring or favorite pendant on a delicate chain works well.

Hold the string or chain with your forefinger and thumb, so that the ring on the chain hangs about 4-5 inches and can swing freely. It helps to anchor your elbow on the table so that you can hold your hand steady.

Calibrate first by letting the pendulum hang and thinking "Yes" or "Show me a positive response." Usually after a few seconds the pendulum will swing back-

and-forth. Next, repeat this step while thinking "No" or "Show me a negative response." Usually the pendulum will swing side-to-side. If you want you can repeat the steps with "I don't know" and "Maybe" responses. Usually the pendulum will swing in a circle, clockwise for one answer and counter clockwise for the other.

To use the pendulum to receive intuitive guidance, relax and quiet your mind by breathing slowly and deeply. Let the pendulum hang still while focusing on your question. Make sure you word your question so that it can be answered with a "yes" or "no". Avoid "should" questions. Don't force it. Just remain relaxed, let go of expectations and notice which way the pendulum swings.

Notice What You Notice

Intuition communicates through what you notice. There is a reason you notice what you do and don't notice something else. . Everything you notice has significance. For example, when you were planning on buying a car, you probably noticed cars, car dealers, car magazines, what cars your friends drive and so forth. Noticing is searching for an answer to the question, "What car shall I buy?" Getting meaning from your intuition is, in part, knowing what question the information you are noticing is answering. The impressions you get don't have to make sense with one another and they may even be contradictory. This is normal.

Understanding Intuitive "Answers"

Understanding the meaning of mental pictures and associations involves translating, interpretation and piecing impressions together. Capturing the sense and impressions you get in response to your question is important. Don't discount or dismiss anything, however irrelevant it may seem. Nothing is irrelevant. Assume all thoughts, senses, feelings, memories are meaningful. Then call on your logical mind to fill in gaps and interpret the symbolic language.

As your skill grows—and it will grow quickly once you give it permission and practice a little—you'll be able to enlist more of your capabilities in achieving high performance goals, because behind goals are choices and behind choices are questions.

Chapter 6

The Avoidance Trap

You are probably reading this book because you want to get moving. Goals are used to motivate and help you to get moving. High performance goals get you into motion and keep moving like a perpetual motion machine. Unfortunately, a lot of people, maybe you, too, have acquired a habitual avoidance motivational style. To achieve negative goals, which, as we shall see, exert a repellent force, you must whip yourself to get into motion and to keep moving.

Kinds of Motivation

There are two types of motivation. "Avoidance motivation", where your motive is getting away from something negative, is the most common. The second kind of motivation is "seeking motivation" which is a moving towards motivation and occurs when you are striving for a positive.

Essential Ingredients

Two ingredients are essential to maintain a high level of motivation—whether seeking or avoidance. Without these essential ingredients you will become increasingly demotivated and, eventually, give up. The first ingredient essential to staying motivated is a "win", which is a positive pay off, reward, or reinforcement. The second essential ingredient is a sense of control over what happens to you.

Wins

There are two kinds of wins—a positive win and a negative win. A positive win occurs when you do something and something positive is turned on or comes to you as a result. For example, you do good work and your supervisor says, "Hey that is a good job". Another example would be dieting and then finding out that you have actually lost weight. Both are examples of positive wins.

Positive wins can be things you get, like a bonus in your paycheck or a special gift. They can be feelings, like joy or a sense of satisfaction. They can be comments from other people, like a compliment. They can be your own thoughts, such as affirmations and patting yourself on the back.

A negative win occurs when a negative situation exists and you do something that turns it off, or takes it away, or makes it better. A reduction in negatives is a win. For example, if you have a headache, which is negative and you take an aspirin and the headache goes away. Feeling better is a "negative win". Not getting additional work by looking busy when your supervisor walks by is a negative win for looking busy. We can think of lots of negative wins. Not getting a speeding ticket because you slowed down after seeing the Highway Patrol car hiding behind a bush is a negative win.

The Avoidance Trap

The problem with avoidance motivation is that it requires a negative to avoid, without which there is no motivation. Some people's entire motivational lives are rooted in this dynamic. In fact, our whole system teaches us avoidance motivation. Studying to *not* fail, working hard to *not* lose your job, driving safely to *not* get a ticket, and not speaking up to *avoid* rejection are a few examples. Motivation is stimulated by having to turn off a negative. You can't get moving unless you have something negative to avoid.

So you avoid—you procrastinate and then use guilt to get moving. You must whip and belittle yourself to keep motivated. The worse thing about avoidance motivation is that when there is not a negative to avoid, you can't get moving. This makes seeking motivation difficult because it involves reaching for a positive instead of turning off a negative. If you are like a lot of people, you turn positives into negatives, then pile on guilt to get yourself motivated. Clearly this is a sub-optimal process that keeps you in a diminished state. Even if you are accomplishing a lot, you are not operating at your highest performance capacity. As an organism, as a spirit, as an individual, you are not functioning in your highest performance mode. Think of what you could achieve if you could soar free of negative constraints.

Sense of Control

Having a sense of control—a feeling that what you do determines your success or failure has a big impact on motivation. We have all experienced times where we worked hard yet kept losing. It is not the losing that is so disheartening but the sense that there is nothing you can do, that no matter how hard you work or how well you perform, you will still lose, generates a "why bother?" attitude. Setting a goal is a way of taking control. You see yourself successfully completing the steps to the goal your sense of empowerment grows and so does your motivation.

Use Your Compass

Negative goals are insidious. You probably make them without realizing their dangers. Sometimes they are foisted on you, like certain performance goals at work. We are all experienced in avoidance motivation, which is imprisoning. It imprisons your spirit; it diminishes and disempowers you.

You can get out of this vicious cycle to become high performance being. Your Intuitive Compass can help you find ways to a high performance life where you function at your optimal capability without wearing yourself down. Instead of forcing and pushing yourself, you can move forward with enthusiasm, stamina and creativity.

Imagine you are walking through the wilderness, forging your path toward your goal and you come a crossroad. Check your Intuitive Compass. Are you acting on attraction? Or repulsion?

When you are worried or confused about a choice, check your Intuitive Compass. For each alternative, imagine yourself actually being in the future situation. Make it as real as you can, then check your Compass. How does this future feel? Will this choice move you towards burnout or towards bliss? Remember to use your wellbeing rating scale also. Still yourself, tune in to your intuition. Notice hunches, and thoughts that come to mind. Perhaps you notice a tiny voice, "This is great!" or "This is not for me."

Does imaging being in this situation or carrying out this action empower and infuse you with enthusiasm? Or does it depress and diminish you? If you don't read one more word of this book, develop your Intuitive Compass. Goals are an incredibly useful tool but you don't have to use goals live a wonderful life! You can use your Intuitive Compass to follow your yellow brick road. If at every choice point you check your Compass, and move in the blissful direction, you will have an amazing journey.

Chapter 7

Powerful Goals

A goal is a target to shoot at. It is a result toward which effort is directed. It is an outcome to be achieved. Usually a goal is a statement of what you want to achieve, but goals can also be unstated and implicit. Goals focus your efforts because there is a target to shoot for. They tell you where to shoot and which way to go.

Suppose, for example, you want to practice archery but have no target. So you shoot into the air, at nothing in particular. Without the target your learning is likely to be slow and your progress poor.

Besides showing you where to shoot, goals provide immediate feedback, which is important in learning. Suppose again, while practicing archery you shoot at the target but cannot see where the arrow hits. Without feedback on your shot, your learning will probably be slow. Suppose six months after you shoot the arrow, you are told that it hit the second ring. This delayed feedback will not be of much assistance in helping you improve your shot.

Powerful goals give immediate feedback on your shot. The sooner the feedback, the more powerful because it is from information about your miss that you can correct your next shot.

Powerful Goals Create a Picture

Vaguely defined goals such as "improving communications," "increasing satisfaction," or "having more fun," for example, are difficult, perhaps impossible to achieve because they don't provide a clear picture of the target—the result you're shooting at. What does "improved communication" look like? How do you know when you've achieved it? Communications with whom? If you talk about politics with your teenaged son after dinner, is that improved communications? Or does improved communications mean you respond to email faster? If so, how much faster? How long, how much and what quality of communication, with whom must be achieved before you can say your communications have improved?

Vaguely stated goals are frustrating because without a clear picture of the target you can miss hitting it. Do this a few times and you can feel that you are constantly falling short in life. To be powerful, the target must be clear enough that you can see yourself achieving the goal.

Use Intuition

Suppose you say, "My goal is to be more cooperative." What do you do? How do you start? To reach your goal, you must know what the hoped for result looks like. Here's where intuition can help. Using your imagination turns intuition on. Imagining your goal creates a mental picture of it. The clearer the picture, and the more magnetic its draw, the better the goal can serve as a target so you can see what you are shooting for. At the same time your intuition actively works at directing your attention in beneficial ways so that things, information, and people appear as you need them, almost magically, when they were probably there all along and you just didn't notice.

The more that you are able to see yourself achieving the goal, the greater its power. For example, "having more fun" can be translated into a specific picture, such as you laughing with friends while playing volleyball at the beach. You see yourself being in such a scene and try it on to notice how it feels being there.

You can picture almost anything in your imagination. You can go into the future or into the past. You can re-write history. You can stretch things, squeeze them, and get inside them. Your imagination is a fantastic tool for managing yourself and deciding where you are going and what you are going to do.

Be Specific

A specific goal describes *what you will be doing* when you achieve your goal—when you're in the "goal-state" which is the time in the future when you have achieved the goal. It is the solution to the problem you are solving, or a milestone you're striving to reach or an end-point in your project, or the achievement of something specific.

Go to the "doing level" of your goal. The doing level is seeing what you are actually doing when you've reached your goal. It includes actions, thoughts and feelings. Going to the doing level makes it easier to create a compelling picture.

How to Go to the Doing Level

Close your eyes and breathe deeply until you feel calm and relaxed. Now *picture yourself in the goal-state*—that time in the future when you have achieved your goal. Don't worry about *how* you'll achieve the goal; just imagine the time when the goal has been achieved. Don't force it. Just wait and allow an image of you at the time you achieve your goal to come to mind. When an image does come to mind, don't judge it. Simply study it. Get to know it.

What does being in the goal-state look like? What are you doing? Who else is there? What are they doing? What resources are used? What money? What people are involved? What technology? Study the details of the image of you in the goal-state.

List everything you saw when imagining yourself in the goal-state—especially those things you didn't expect. Make sure to describe how you *felt* and what you were doing.

Repeat the exercise several times until you have created 5 or 6, or more, pictures of yourself having achieved your goal. For example, when imagining the goal of "having fun," you might make it more specific by seeing yourself in a comfortable chair enjoying the warmth of a fire in your fireplace. In another scene you might see yourself arranging beautiful flowers from your garden in a vase. Another picture of having fun might be seeing yourself chatting on the phone with a good friend.

Goals have markers or milestones, sometimes called subgoals or objectives, along the way to the realization of the ultimate end and actualization of what you are seeking. As we will see later, breaking goals into small steps makes them more manageable and easier to achieve. The same principles we're discussing here apply to these minigoals. Just as your ultimate goals should be powerful, so, too, your mini-goals will be easier to achieve if they are powerful.

In addition to creating pictures of your end-goal, use compelling pictures to pull you towards your mini-goals. For example, if you were striving to get your masters degree (end-goal) you can create pictures of what you will be doing when you have a job requiring your degree and seeing your name on your business card with M.S. after it. You can also create pictures of the small steps you must take to get the masters degree, such as seeing yourself looking at the acceptance letter, or seeing yourself discussing your thesis with a professor.

Try It On

This simple envisioning exercise allows you to "try on" possible goals to see how they fit. Ask the question, "What will I be doing when I . . .?" Remember, asking a question activates intuition. Patiently wait for an image to come to mind. Your intuition will give information about how the goal fits you.

Remember, to be powerful, the goal must be a good fit like a comfortable shoe; otherwise you could be hobbled and unable to get anywhere. Notice sensations you experience when you imagine being in the goal-state.  If it doesn't feel good, then change the picture until it does feel good. Experiment to discover what fits you. Work on the image of the goal-state until you find pictures where you feel energized and "one" with what you're doing. Use your Intuitive Compass. Keep refining your pictures until your Compass points towards bliss.

At first, it may be hard to keep your rational mind from doing its thing—judging. "That's no good!" "You should . . .!" or conjuring up "politically correct" pictures that may look good but don't necessarily fit you all that well. When this happens don't argue, just notice the thought and then set it aside.

A powerful goal is clear about what you will be doing when you achieve it. The more specifically you describe what you will be doing when you achieve the goal, the easier it is to create pictures of you doing it, the clearer your target will be. A clear target tells you where to aim and what to do and kicks in your intuition, which makes achieving your goal a lot easier.

Powerful Goals are Magnetic

How your subconscious responds to a goal greatly influences its power. You need a compelling image to pull you towards the goal; otherwise you must push yourself towards it. As soon as you push on yourself, resistance emerges. It's a natural response like putting out your hand when you fear you are about to fall or like your dog resisting when you pull on his collar.

Compelling goals are easier to achieve because they are positive. For one thing the brain processes positive information faster than negative information, which probably explains why double negatives are so confusing. Consider the following: "I've never resisted that" or "Don't not call if you'll be late." Such statements make us stop and shake our heads in confusion while we attempt to decipher their meaning.

Along the same lines, if you say to a young child, "Don't touch that vase", the child is likely to go straight for it. Why? Telling the child not to touch the vase creates an image of touching the vase in the child's mind! The same is true of your subconscious. For example, consider the imperative "Don't think of a pink elephant." What comes to mind? If you're like most people, an image of a pink elephant is in your mind while you attempt to *not* think of it. Like the child, the subconscious responds to images, and tends to delete negative modifiers.

Attractive vs Repulsive Goals

The purpose of a goal is to motivate—to get you moving. It is easier to get moving when the picture of you in the goal-state is compelling. Then the goal draws you toward it, like a magnet does.

Thinking of your goal brings its attractive or repulsive properties to mind. The trick in creating a magnetic goal—a goal that draws you toward it—is in specifying the goal in such a way that the images it brings to mind attract you. Attractive images attract. They are compelling and draw you to them. Compelling goals kick in seeking motivation.

A goal like "losing weight by not eating sweets", for example, is negative and contains a hidden suggestion that continually reminds you of what you want to *not do*—eat sweets. This kicks in avoidance motivation. A positive statement can be discovered by imagining what you will be *doing* when you have lost weight. For example, it might be "looking good in a size 12 bathing suit". Seeing yourself looking good in a bathing suit is more compelling, hence more motivating, than imagining *not* eating sweets. Your journey towards a smaller waistline is more joyful when you are seeking to wear a size 12, than when your are avoiding eating delicious sweets.

Another example might be "to manage time better by setting priorities" which conjures up a ho-hum image at best. Worse, you might see yourself with clipboards and checklists, which are probably repulsive images and sets avoidance motivation into motion. A goal with a more compelling image might be "to spend at least one weekend a month in my lakeside cabin" which is what you will be doing when you have become a better time manager. Imagining yourself relaxing at your cabin is more compelling than imaging making lists and checking them twice! Yet, to actually carve out the free time to go to your cabin might involve making lists, but doing so is not the picture of where you are going, it is just an intermediary step you must take to get there.

Negative Goals Repel

Goals that contain negative targets are surprisingly common. Sometimes the goal was imposed on you by an authority like a parent or teacher. Other times the goal appears positive until you check your Intuitive Compass to discover that the doing level of the goal promotes burnout, not bliss. Negative goals put you in a conflict situation, because success is defined in terms of activities or changes you dislike. Achieving such goals is difficult. You will probably fail to achieve the goal because the picture it elicits repels you.

Some goals sound positive but contain hidden negative images. Sybil, an artist, said her goal was "to increase billings by ten thousand dollars a year". On the face of it, this seems like a positive goal. Asked how she felt when biding her clients more money, she admitted that she felt tremendously uncomfortable. This means that to reach her goal, Sybil must do something she doesn't like doing several times a year. If each biding were increased by $100, assuming every bid is accepted, she would have to give 100 such bids in the following year to achieve her goal. That's almost two times a week! The mental picture of giving higher bids was repugnant to Sybil and made her anxious just thinking about it. To achieve her goal, Sybil would have to push herself relentlessly. Goals with hidden negatives like this thrust you into a cycle of self-prodding, resistance and negativity.

Jeff, a plastic surgeon who ran a small clinic, had a similar dilemma. His goal was "to plan and implement eight marketing strategies in the coming year." Again the goal seemed positive, until Jeff described how he felt about selling. He cringed as he said he didn't like it at all! Marketing one's business is selling. So like Sybil, Jeff's seemingly positive goal was actually negative because it required him to sell himself which he doesn't like doing.

If Sybil and Jeff are to achieve their goals they must find compelling images and restate their goals to elicit them when they think of their goals.

Powerful Goals Say When

Timelines help you to bring the pieces together. Goals with no specific completion date make setting timelines for action steps difficult. Such open-ended goals undermine motivation and encourage procrastination. But a deadline must be realistic if the goal is to be powerful. Unrealistically short deadlines can trigger panic, provoking the opposite "Why bother?" attitude, and generally generate an oppressive climate. A deadline that is too short is usually better than no deadline at all. Unrealistic deadlines usually become apparent quickly, providing you an opportunity to readjust them to a more realistic time frame.

Chapter 8

Use Magnetism

Not all targets are the same. Some are easier to hit. Some are more fun, while others are dull and boring. Compelling targets have a magnetic force that pulls your efforts toward them, making them easier to hit. Many factors add to the magnetism of a goal to make it more compelling.

Engage Your Senses

Make your goal vibrant and alive by engaging all your senses. Research has demonstrated that when more senses are engaged, more of the brain is used. As it is used the brain's wiring actually grows by developing thicker stems, or axons, and creating more complex connections, called synapses, between the cells. What this means is that what you think about and what you imagine establishes neural pathways which are reinforced each time you imagine that picture again.

Add Sensory Images

A goal-picture such as seeing yourself playing volleyball with friends on the beach can be made more compelling by imaging the sounds of the ocean waves, the seagulls cawing, your friends laughing and the slapping sound when hitting the ball. Add in the sense of touch.

Feel the grainy sand under your feet and the weight of the ball as you throw it up to serve it. Luxuriate in the warm sun on your head and back. Notice a refreshing breeze caressing your cheek. Smell the salty air and the faint scent of perspiration. Taste the refreshing flavor of the cold beer as you gulp it down during the break. Add lots of visual details. See a blue sky with wispy clouds forming in the west. Notice what you and your friends are wearing. See the volleyball coming towards you. Notice the brand name written on the side of the ball as you hold it between plays. See your car parked up on the road.

Imagine your goal-picture often, each time add more sensory details to make the picture robust. Don't limit yourself to external details. Notice how you feel inside. What is your emotional state? Pay particular attention to joyful emotions, which add tremendously to the goal's magnetism. Remember to use your Intuitive Compass and discard details that turn your Compass towards burnout.

Just "flashing" on your goal-picture, or imaging it for a few seconds, sends impulses along neural pathways established when you first began creating your picture.

Enlist Your Values

Meaningfulness is a tremendously important factor in a goal's magnetism. Something with meaning has special significance for you. It is something you find worthwhile and important. Studies show that people who say that they are happy say it's because they are pursuing something meaningful. We want to feel we are spending our time—our lives—doing something important—something that matters. Meaningfulness makes the heart sing. Goals that are attuned to your values have meaning, which increases their magnetism.

How to Clarify Values

Clarifying values helps in developing goals that fit you well. Start by looking at things you love doing. Having one's own ski school sounds like a natural goal if you love skiing and have been a ski bum all your life, traveling around the world working the ski patrol. But maybe not! If what you really love about being a ski bum is the vagabond lifestyle, then the picture of running a school could be repellent because, even though you can ski everyday, you'll be tied down, doing bookkeeping, and supervising employees. What this example illustrates is that what is really important may not always be readily apparent, and your values may conflict with one another.

Dig below the surface. About something you love doing, ask yourself, "What do I love about this?" "What about this really matters to me?" Don't try to force an answer. Instead, quiet your mind and allow your intuition to speak to you. Be receptive and notice what thoughts occur and what images come to mind. When an image comes to mind, ask of it, "What do I love about this?" "What about this really matters to me?" Continue asking, "What do I love about this?" of the thoughts and images that come until you feel you've found what is most meaningful about the activity. What do these images and thoughts have in common? Where's the spirit?

A Big Bag of Gold

Seeker: I need a job. How can I find meaningful work?

Shaman Woman: I have two jobs that need doing. In one, you do nothing and get paid a big bag of gold. In the second, you work long and hard and get only one gold coin. Which job do you want?

Seeker: The one that pays the big bag of gold!

Shaman Woman: Okay, go and sit in that room. At the end of the month I will give you a big bag of gold.

Seeker: There's only an empty desk and a chair in there. What is my job? What am I to do?

Shaman Woman: You must do nothing.

The next day the Seeker hurriedly ran up to the Shaman Woman.

Seeker: Can I have the second job—the hard job that pays only one gold coin?

Shaman Woman: But the job you have pays a big bag of gold.

Seeker: Yes, but I'm doing nothing. I can't stand it! Please let me have the difficult job.

Shaman Woman: Okay! Okay! See that pile of wood? Chop it. See that bucket? Fill it from the well. Take the wood and the water to the orphanage so the children can have hot food and warm baths.

The Seeker worked long hours chopping wood and carrying water. His muscles ached every night. At the end of the month the Shaman Woman brought his pay.

> *Shaman Woman:* You have worked hard and your
>   pay is only one gold coin. Aren't you
>   sorry you left the job that paid a big bag
>   of gold?
> *Seeker:* No, I would never trade the smiles of the
>   children for a bag of gold.

Meaningfulness is the domain of intuition. Intuition takes the details and finds meaning in them by grasping the big picture. Dreary and menial activities can be made more meaningful when they tie into your values and life's purpose.

Tie into Your Life's Purpose

Many people don't know why they are living the life they lead and doing the things they do. They don't think of themselves as having a purpose. As a result, they feel lost, a drift, helpless, and at the whim of a senseless world.

The human spirit has a hungering for meaning. "Why" is one of the first questions a child embraces. "Why, Daddy?" "Why does the moon shine?" "Why do dogs bark?" "Why do I sleep?" "Why?" "Why?" "Why?" A life's purpose is an all-encompassing answer to the question, "Why?" It is the "reason" for your being here. It inspires and motivates you to make strides in the direction you set for yourself.

Your purpose is as unique as you are. When you get in touch with having a "purpose" you will experience a greater sense of control in your life. Looking at your daily moments through the lens of your life purpose provides inspiration—it brings spirit into your life—from which you can gather motivation. It provides a context for your dreams to come true. Hitching on to your life's purpose provides direction, helps organize your efforts and gives you something to measure your progress against. In short, you are the pilot in this adventure called "your life". Your life's purpose is completely in your hands. No one else can determine the direction of your life, unless you turn yourself over to them.

Organize your goals around your life's purpose. You don't have to have a once-and-forever purpose. You can use a short-term purpose to give a direction and jump-start you into action. You can alter, shape, modify or get a completely new purpose later.

How do you recognize your purpose—your reason for being? It is not the action itself but the justification for doing it—the force and driving energy that moves you. Notice what your passions are. This is another clue. What do you enjoy so much that you forget time while doing it? What do you do even though you don't get paid?

Your calling makes itself known by what motivates you, past and present, by what attracts you, by what you resist, by what frustrates you. It can be identified in glimpses of what you admire in others.

Pursue Your Destiny

Your destiny is your journey this time around. It is the path you forge as you achieve your goals and fulfill your life's purpose. Destiny is not a point in the future. You don't find it wandering aimlessly. Your destiny begins the moment you act. Your destiny is your way of life. Your destiny is an exciting journey that is always in progress, not just a final destination. It is the sum total of your life decisions and the goals you've pursued.

The time to live fully is right now. Live the life you truly want to live. Your happiness will flow from striving. You experience the full power of your destiny by exercising the power of your talents and the free will that you have been given.

Deciding upon your destiny is akin to daydreaming, only with a productive agenda. Spend time imagining the rewards you receive as your destiny unfolds. What do you desire? What would you love doing? What do you long to have, to do, to contribute, to accomplish, and to experience. As you think of things you want to do, write them down. What have you always wanted to experience? Keep a list of these gems. Your destiny will most likely flow from something you love to do that serves others.

Think of your goals as stepping-stones to achieving your life's purpose as you pursue your destiny and you will experience a wonderful sense of empowerment. Try it.

Chapter 9

Mapping the Steps

Having a map makes it easier to get where you want to go because it shows your route and where to expect obstacles.

Strange as it may seem, the most effective way to map the route to your goal is to begin at the end, with a picture of your destination—your goal completed—and work backwards to where you are now.

Begin at the End

To reach your goal take small steps beginning with what you can do right now, because a journey of a thousand miles begins with a first step in the here and now.

We create things and get places by imagining the finished project—what it looks like—and working backward to where one can begin. Think about it. When you build something, like a deck, you make a drawing first, put in measurements, figure out and purchase materials needed, and then begin building your deck. You don't build a house, for example, by amassing a load of lumber and then building a corner wall.

Discover the Steps

Take your goal apart to discover the small steady action steps you must take to reach your destination. Barbara Sher, author of *Wishcraft: How to Get What You Really*

Want has developed a simple technique. Here's how: Imagine your goal and ask, "Can I do this now?" If the answer is "No," then ask, "What do I have to do first?" Write your answer down. Of this step again ask, "Can I do this now?" If you can't do it now, then ask, "What do I have to do first?" and write the answer down. Continue in this manner until you've identified all of the steps that you must take to get to your goal.

Turn Steps into Objectives

Objectives are tools that make it easier to carry out the steps you must take to achieve your goal. An objective is a statement of what you plan to accomplish at each step. The more thought out and carefully phrased your objective, the easier it is to make the step. Objectives are easier to meet when they describe the results to be achieved, have a completion date and are measurable.

What Results Will You Achieve?

Objectives help you keep your eye on the destination. A well-stated objective describes what, not how. In writing out objectives, describe what situation will exist when you complete the step, but not how you will do it. "The fifth chapter will be completed and approved by the editor," or "The books will be sorted and boxed up," or "I will be able to lift 50 pounds at the gym."

How Will You Measure Progress?

Concentrating on results provides a concrete marker for evaluating your progress. It is important that you can measure results because measurability enables you to know when you've completed each step. Long-distance runners aiming for a ten-mile marker, for example, would have difficulty telling when they've reached it without a mileage counter or a signpost.

When stating your objective make sure to include to what degree, how long, how far, or how fast you must perform to adequately complete the step. With a little creativity you can measure almost anything. For example, rating scales, such as a scale from 1 to 5, with 5 being very high and 1 being very low, can be used to measure emotions, like joyfulness, and bodily sensations, like anxiety. Another approach is to count how often you have particular thoughts or how often particular events occur before and after taking the step, for example.

Stating steps in a way that your progress can be measured lets you know how close you are to completing each. It is motivating and builds confidence and feelings of control to see yourself getting closer to the mark.

Is It Attainable?

Objectives that make you stretch a little are good, but objectives that you cannot attain are frustrating and diminish motivation. Instead of demanding a giant step, set a series of goals that stretch you bit-by-bit; don't demanding the impossible.

When Will You Complete It?

A completion date or deadline provides a clear point in time to achieve the result. The completion date enables you to schedule activities and to pace yourself. Like the other elements of an objective, the completion date can be motivating if it is realistic, or discouraging if it is unrealistic. If you fall behind, the completion date reveals this quickly so that you can take corrective action before things get hopeless.

Take Small Steps

If you are like many people, you often have trouble getting started toward your goal. The problem is inertia. In physics, the principle of inertia states that a body at rest tends to stay at rest. The moment before you start

you are a body at rest! To take a first step, you must
break your inertia to get moving. Many people
defeat themselves by demanding way too
much, which is overwhelming and
can paralyze their efforts, es-   p e -
cially in the beginning.   T h e
secret to getting   started and
keeping your   momentum going is to   take small steps.
                    No step is too small.
            What is important is maintaining
         a steady momentum. Once you are
      moving the law of inertia—a body in motion
   tends to stay in motion—helps you to keep going.

Keep Starting

The single most important action for success is making a beginning. To make a beginning, you must know
how to start. Breaking something into very small steps
helps. Don't demand a lot, just take a small step and
you've started. For example, making a list is a small step
and gets you started.

It is easy to get sidetracked or distracted. Sometimes
there are emergencies that force you to put everything
aside so that your progress comes to a halt. It is inevi-
table that you will plateau and peter out. Don't worry
about this. Instead expect it and plan for it. What sepa-
rates high performance goal achievers from moderate
performers is that high performance folks begin again and
again.

Set Yourself Up to Win

Steps should only be as big as you *know* you can
achieve with relative ease. If a step is something particularly difficult—because it is distasteful, involves an en-
trenched habit or requires a new skill—break it into
smaller steps. For example, suppose you want to stop
smoking. If, As the first step, you demand that, for a

month, you will chew gum every time you feel like smoking, you are likely to fail. Chances for success are better if you reduce the time to only one day, instead. When you achieve that, make your next step for a slightly longer period of time, for example.

The objective helps you get started and keep your momentum going. Set yourself up to succeed. Set objectives you *know you can meet.*

Stretch Yourself

Although objectives should be small steps, they should be big enough to make you stretch. Think of yoga as an example. When doing yoga, you position your body into a posture and then slowly stretch the muscles you are exercising. Don't worry about the steps being too small as long as there is some small stretch. Remember the inertia principle: "A body in motion tends to stay in motion." Use small steps to keep yourself in motion toward your goal.

Make Getting There Fun

People often equate self-management or self-discipline with austerity, sacrifice and pain. Such an approach is a mistake and undermines success. Grease the wheels of change with fun. Enjoyment of a task lessens the toil of doing it. Consider physical exercise, for example. Doing jumping jacks and running in place isn't much fun. By comparison, playing tennis with a friend is more fun and provides a good workout. With this in mind, think of ways you can build fun into the process of achieving your goals.

Chapter 10

Program Your Goals

Your rational mind is at the helm when you are awake; when sleeping, however, the balance of power shifts as the quiet mind comes forth. It is during dreaming, as well as when you are deeply relaxed, that you can most easily plant your goal—imprint it—at a deeper level of mind.

Enlist Your Dreams

Dreams are mysterious, seeming to come of their own accord. They can be confusing, even frightening at times. Most people dream four or five times a night. During sleep the brain goes in and out of something called "REM" (rapid eye movement) when the brain emits a particular kind of brain wave. It is during REM sleep that dreams occur.

You can enlist your dreams to help achieve your goals. Answers to questions and solutions to problems often come into your awareness through your dreams, when your rational mind's tight hold is loosened. There is nothing new or "new age" about this. Indigenous people, like American Indians, Eskimos and the Senoi—a native people studied by Dr. Patricia Garfield, have traditionally looked to dreams for guidance in important decisions.

Examining dreams for answers is an age-old approach to solving problems. Just before the Battle of Little Big

Horn, for example, the Indian Chief, Sitting Bull, had a dream in which he saw warriors winning a big battle. Trusting the message, Sitting Bull sent his braves against Col. Custer who they defeated.

Not only can you get answers from dreams but also dreams have a carry-over effect into daily life. Garfield reports in *Creative Dreaming* that you can shape your dream state into a supportive level of consciousness to favorably influence what happens when you are awake.

Garfield's research shows that dreams can serve as critical learning experiences. Since your quiet mind is in control when asleep, the learning takes place at a nonconscious level. The implications are quite fascinating. Dreams might act as a blue print for possible futures, for example.

The quiet brain is the doorway to your intuitive self and dreams provide an opening to reach inward. What this means is that during dreaming you can program your goal, at an intuitive level, so that the thrust to achieve it is embraced by your subconscious. The result is that most things you do will fold into achieving your goal almost synergistically. You don't have to "think" about it and drive yourself toward it.

This doesn't mean you should abandon the linear techniques of the rational mind, like writing lists, setting objectives and measuring progress. What it means is that by programming your goals (and sub-goals or small steps) at this deeper level, you enlist more of your capability in service of the goal. It means you function at a high performance level, with all systems working together synergistically, instead of fighting and whipping yourself along. Although you must still work hard and may be frequently challenged, you move through your steps "naturally", without stress, self-doubts and internal struggle. Of course, the nature of your goal may create struggle with the world out there, but inside you are confident with your intent so that you can focus more fully on achieving it.

Shape Your Dreams

We shape our dreams all the time without realizing it. Probably you have had the experience of an event during the day appearing in a dream in strange ways that night.

You can learn to control your dreams in helpful ways. You can give yourself suggestions that manifest during dreams, for example. You can induce dreams about specific issues. Attitude about dreams is very important. Your mental state immediately prior to sleep is especially critical. You must value dreams and believe in them.

Keep a Dream Diary

The first step in gaining more control over your dreams, so that you can enlist their help, is to simply become more aware of them. People differ in dream recallability. With practice you can learn to recall your dream adventures. As your skill grows it becomes easier to remember your dreams.

The best time to practice dream recall is in the morning after waking up naturally, without the disruption of an alarm. Jumping out of bed disrupts memories of dreams because dream memories last about five minutes, after which they quietly drift away.

Don't open your eyes. Lie still with eyes closed and let images flow into your mind. When a snippet of a dream comes, review it and try to recall the scene just before it, then the preceding one and the scene preceding that one. Record everything in your dream diary.

Lying quietly in a favorite sleep position, then gently moving to another sleep position can sometimes stimulate additional recall. Usually more images come.

Keep a dream diary in which you describe your dreams in as much detail as you can remember, including the feelings and emotions you experienced. You might keep a pad, pen and pen-size flashlight next to your bed so that you can record dreams when you wake up in the night.

After keeping a dream diary for few months, you'll notice that certain symbols appear again and again. Pay particular attention when you encounter one of your dream symbols in your waking life. For example, suppose owls appear often in your dreams. If you see an owl in a painting, a TV commercial, a magazine, child's book, for example, pay attention, especially if you have been asking for intuitive advice and there is anything seemingly co-incidental about it. Maybe there is message. Remember intuition works in part by directing your attention. Noticing symbols that have personal significance is one way this happens.

How to Incubate a Dream

Your mind is more receptive to suggestions when you are relaxed. Use this principle to incubate a dream. Make yourself comfortable in a safe place and arrange to be uninterrupted.

Relax First

Kick off your shoes and loosen any tight clothing, like your belt or a buttoned up collar. Breathe in deeply and slowly through your nose until you notice the fullness in your chest, then slowly exhale through your mouth. Just continue breathing slowly and deeply in and out while focusing on the sensations of your breathe. Imagine that your breath is a continuous loop, with the in and out phases being of the same length and very smooth.

Suggest a Dream

When you feel calm and relaxed, formulate the subject of your intended dream. Concentrate on only one desired dream topic, especially in the beginning. You might say to yourself, "I want a dream to tell me what to do about —" or "I want a dream to show me how to feel better about —." or "I want a dream of flying." for example. Alternatively you might imagine yourself having achieved your goal and suggest that you will have a dream around that picture of the future.

Some people experience success by praying to their angels or to God for particular help to come through a dream. Dr. Doreen Virtue, author of *Divine Guidance*, suggests a prayer something like, "Please enter my dreams tonight and give me guidance about —. I ask that you help me remember these ideas when I awake and clear away the fears that hold me back."

Your suggestion should be definite, brief and positive. "Tonight I dream of living in a home I love" is better than "I think I'll try to have a dream about getting a house," for example. Concentrate on your suggestion or prayer right before sleep.

You must believe that you can influence your dreams. Focus your attention patiently and persistently on the desired dream. Sometimes it helps to imagine yourself actually in the dream you hope to have later when you are asleep.

Avoid Drugs and Drink

Sleeping pills and alcohol interfere with dreaming and should be avoided when you want to incubate a dream. The brain hormone, melatonin, aids natural sleep and promotes dreaming. Melatonin is created by the body, but its production declines with age and can be hampered by many environmental pollutants which accounts for why older people often have trouble sleeping and claim to rarely dream.

Kava Root extract also promotes dreaming and acts synergistically when taken with melatonin. Both are available in most health food stores.

Use Your Dreams

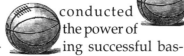

A fascinating study conducted in the late 1970s revealed the power of practicing a skill, like making successful basketball shots, in one's imagination. The researchers trained three groups, all properly matched to control for things like age, sex and basketball throwing ability. One group physically practiced throwing baskets from the centerline. The second group sat on the gym floor and imagined throwing baskets. The third group did something.

Just as we would expect, the study showed that practice definitely helps to build basketball-throwing skill. On final tests the group that did not practice performed the worst. However, the interesting result was that there was no difference in final test scores between the group that physically practiced and the one that only imagined practicing making baskets.

Dreaming is super-powered imagination. It feels real. Garfield's research shows that dream work influences your emotions and performance during waking life.

You can enlist your dreams to learn skills needed to achieve your goals. Be specific in your pre-dream instructions and concentrate on actually seeing yourself achieving your goal, or carrying out a small step towards it.

Interpreting Dream Messages

Dreams are filled with odd images and common daily events woven together in unexpected ways. Gleaning their meaning is an art and skill that improves with practice.

One approach is to carry on a conversation, one at a time with each dream character or symbol in the dream. The best time to try this is when you are still in a drowsy state in bed in morning. Picture one of your dream images and ask it questions like: Who are you? Why do you do such and such? Don't hurry. Wait and listen. Be receptive. Notice feelings that come. Don't demand a particular "answer". Just notice the thoughts and hunches that come to you. Answers received during this unique way of talking to yourself can be unexpected and informative. As you become skilled in questioning dream images, you will find yourself receiving more helpful information during your dreams.

Use Relaxation

When you are deeply relaxed, the rational mind with its defenses, recede and, like in dreaming, the quiet mind comes forth. This is when you have the greatest access to your intuitive self and are the most influenced by your suggestion.

Many people feel a little apprehensive because they have heard that deep relaxation is akin to "hypnosis", which brings up fears of someone making you do something you don't like and that may be humiliating. Rest assured that your intuitive self is constantly watching out for you and is not going to go along with anything that is not in your best interest.

Relax yourself deeply. When you feel quite calm and are ready—don't rush—imagine yourself carrying out the specific behaviors needed to achieve a particular step to your goal. Alternatively, imagine yourself in the future in that time when you have actually achieved the goal. Take it slowly and build the intensity of your "fantasy". Make it as real and as vivid as you can. Then use the same suggestions you would use to incubate a dream.

Just relax and picture your end-goal (or the small step you are working on) in your imagination. See yourself in that time when you have achieved the goal (or small step). Listen for intuition's tiny voice, those quiet hunches and ideas that seem to come into your mind of their own accord. If the goal, or particular step, you are working on is wrong for you, your intuition will tell you—if you listen. Check your Intuitive Compass and modify the fantasy to move towards bliss. To enlist all your capabilities in high performance goal setting—and achieving your goals—you must trust yourself.

Chapter 11

Build Commitment

There's an old saying: "The road to hell is paved with good intentions." That's because good intentions alone are not enough to propel you through the efforts needed to achieve your goals. You must motivate yourself and have the commitment to carry out those good intentions. One obstacle for many people is the tendency to rebel, even against your own best laid plans, which gets in the way of doing what you want to do. A bigger obstacle may be not knowing how to manage yourself—not knowing how to get yourself moving and keep yourself moving towards your goal.

Make a Deal

A simple technique for fortifying good intentions is called a "self-contract," which is a written agreement with yourself stating what you will do. It is a little like a New Year's resolution because you are resolving to do something. But a self-contract differs from a New Year's resolution in a several notable ways. First, New Year's resolutions tend to be global promises like "I will be more receptive to change," or "I will lose weight and take care of my health," or "I'll be more loving to my family," or "I'll be more successful and make more money." By comparison, a self-contract contains a specific statement of what you are going to do, along with when, where and how long you will do it. "For the next three days I will run one mile before dinner."

Writing down what you want to accomplish solidifies the picture of what you will do in your mind. It focuses your attention and makes the idea more concrete. Your desire is no longer a passive daydream but becomes an action plan.

Include a Payoff

The contract describes the step you will carry out and what reward you will receive when you successfully complete it. It is sometimes called a contingency statement: "When I do X, then I'll get Y." Getting Y, the payoff, is contingent upon performing X. By comparison, if there is a payoff for the New Year's resolution, it is implicit and rarely stated as an if/then contingency statement.

The payoff is a reward you give yourself for fulfilling the terms of the contract. Rewards are vital to motivation and maintaining your momentum towards your goal. Payoffs can be large, like getting yourself a new car when you have met an ambitious financial goal, for example. Also powerful are the small pleasures, like a special dinner out, an evening at the theatre, a new fishing rod, a massage and other things and experiences that you want.

Payoffs can also be little indulgences you already routinely enjoy, like renting a video for evening entertainment, buying a cappuccino, calling a friend, reading the Sports Section in the Sunday paper, watching a favorite TV show, and so forth. Such daily pleasures have potential motivational power you can harness to propel yourself towards your goals. All you do is to make getting the small pleasure contingent upon carrying out some small action that moves you towards your goal.

For example, suppose as a step to your goal of making a transition from living in a big city to a less hectic country area, you want to explore the economic climate in Maine and you have been referred to the Portland Chamber of Commerce website for information. You could make a deal with yourself in which you agree to review the site now, and when you finish to then treat yourself to a cappuccino, which you enjoy having nearly everyday in the mid-morning. By making having the "cap" contingent upon taking a tiny step first, you harness its motivational power. Give yourself lots of small pleasures—and some larger ones, too. Just take a tiny step towards your goal first. With this approach you can almost effortlessly move towards your goal—especially when the steps are very small.

Make a Want List

It helps to make a list of the little pleasures you routinely give yourself, like reading a book, watching TV, listening to a CD, drinking a soda, calling a friend, petting your cat, sitting and relaxing and so forth. Too often, such pleasures are used to procrastinate. "I'll get a soda, then I'll look at that informational website." This is a backward contingency that rewards procrastination. You can turn it around and beat the avoidance trap by carrying out the action before, not after, getting the payoff. The trick is to require only a tiny action, especially in the beginning. Take lots of small steps so that you can give yourself lots of little pleasures. Be generous with yourself—just take a small step first. You'll be amazed at how fast you reach your goals and how easy it will be.

Make it Short-Term

A self-contract has a term or termination date, whereas a New Year's resolution is an open-ended forever demand: "I will stop smoking" as compared to "Today I will not smoke during breakfast." The self-contract teaches you that you *can do* what you commit to doing.

As a result you feel empowered and your self-esteem and confidence grow. By comparison, the open-endedness of a New Year's resolution sets you up to fail. Most smokers don't stop "cold turkey" which is what the resolution demands. If you go a whole week without smoking and then have a single puff, you have failed. In the process you learn that you *can not do* what you decide to do, which engenders a sense of loss of control, with a predictable decline in self-esteem and confidence.

Just a Little Stretch

Make the contract for only as long as you are sure you can stick to it. This might be a week, a day or only an hour. For example, the person running a mile after work might write a new contract to do so for five days. When she accomplishes this step, she is free to renew it or she could expand it to running two miles before dinner, for example. She could expand the terms of the contract, or even abandon the effort and still have succeeded in doing what she determined to do.

Write it Down

Simply writing down what you have decided to do promotes commitment. Sometimes it is helpful to have a friend, co-worker, or mate witness and sign your contract to provide a kind of self-imposed peer pressure. It is surprising how effective this simple tool can be.

Achieving to Be

Many people are trapped in the idea that they can't be happy until they have achieved certain things. Robert Stubert calls it "achieving to be" in *Creating Your Ultimate Destiny*. Unfortunately for many people, shortly after making an achievement, the "high" feeling fades.

Achievement becomes like a drug that requires greater and greater levels to "get high" so that after an achievement they experience happiness briefly, but then must accomplish yet more to be happy again—for a brief time.

When your happiness hinges on achievement you crave ever more achievement, while happiness slips elusively just beyond your fingertips so you are perpetually caught up in struggle, stress, and worry and your life becomes an emotional roller coaster.

Enjoy the Journey

According to Stubert, when you desire things, status or situations, what you actually desire are the feelings you anticipate having when you achieve what you are seeking. If you are striving to become wealthy, for example, what you actually want are the feelings of security, admiration, respect, self-esteem and whatever else you imagine being rich will bring. If you are wishing for a big promotion you may be seeking feelings of power fulfillment and control.

Actually, you can access the feelings you seek right now. It only takes a decision to do so. Try this: Relax and choose an emotion like feeling affection for a dear friend or a beloved pet. Decide for the moment to feel affection, then reach back in your memory to a time when you felt affection for your friend or pet. Project yourself back into the memory, relive the moment and experience what it is like to feel affection. Make the memory as real and vivid as you can—really *feel* the affection now that you felt then.

To prolong the emotion, tell yourself affirmations about it. "Right now I feel so much affection for Pusskat" and think about his particularly endearing qualities, as you summon the feelings of affection into your body again. Emotions are not something that happen to you. Emotions are something that you do. You can choose when to feel affection. You don't have to wait for the feelings you long for to arrive of their own accord. You *can* feel what you choose. You are in control of your emotions, not a victim of them.

You may be striving to acquire wealth, to start a relationship, or advance in your career, for example. You can allow yourself to reap the emotional benefits of your achievements now. When you do, a burden is lifted from you. Instead of struggling to reach goals, you arrive at them. The journey is the experience, arriving at the goal is the destination.

Calling Forth Negative Emotions

Negative emotions, like fear, guilt, anxiety, self-consciousness and so forth are amazingly easy to call forth. If you are like most of us, you can remember an old situation, like your father being especially critical, for example, and telling you how you've failed in some fundamental way. Within seconds you re-experience the quilt, shame and fear you felt at the time—even though it was 20, 30, or even more years ago, and even though your father may even have passed from this lifetime. Negative emotions from the past come quickly forward to occupy the present where you find yourself dwelling upon more recent "guilts". In no time, you feel guilty in the here and now. Most of us are well skilled in making such negative emotional transplantations—whether it is guilt, depression, fear, or anxiety.

Feel Good Now

While you may not be as skilled at doing it, positive emotions can be transplanted in just the same way. You can feel peaceful, contented, joyful, secure and happy right now, without having to achieve something first—to justify feeling good. When happiness is no longer contingent upon reaching your goal you can shift from the worry and struggle of whether you will get there, to experiencing the joy and thrill of the journey.

Some people fear their motivation to achieve will be squashed if they feel good now. It is as if they believe they don't deserve to be happy without proving themselves and earning it. You do not have to wait until you reach your destination to feel good. Focus on the joy of your adventure now, instead of calling forth worry about tomorrow. Without so much negativity and anxiety, motivation increases so that you can achieve more, more quickly, while enjoying it more. A happy mind free of excessive stress and struggle and is open to new possibilities. Happiness breeds clearer vision and optimism to make your journey into the future an exciting and magical adventure instead of a stressful trek.

Language of Commitment

There is an old truism: fake it and you will make it. You can build commitment and confidence by "faking it" and acting "as if" you are committed and confident. One place to start is your language. When you are working on something, do you say, "I'm trying to . . . "? "I am trying to lose weight," Or "I am trying to increase my income," Or "I am trying to start the car." The small word, "trying", can erode commitment, especially if it is already a little shaky. To "try" means to make an attempt to do something, to put out effort, which as of yet has not worked. Hidden in the word trying is a strong suggestion of failure—the car may not start at all and you will probably not lose weight.

Drop "trying" and use the language of commitment instead. It begins with two words: "I am". Statements beginning with "I am" are extremely powerful. In *Conversations with God* by Neale Walsch, God told him that when you make a statement beginning with "I am" you are giving a command to the universe—and the universe will respond accordingly.

Say the following statements aloud: "I am increasing my income." "I am losing weight." "I am starting the car." Notice how much stronger and committed they sound—and you feel—as compared to the statements qualified by "trying". When you use the language of commitment you sound committed, people see you as committed and soon you feel committed.

Enlist Other's Support

When you change, significant others—family members, roommates, and co-workers—are forced to changed whether they want to or not, which can undermine your efforts to better yourself. Suppose, for example, you and your spouse relax by watching videotapes in the evening. However, to advance your career, you enroll in a masters degree program. Now instead of watching videos in the evening, the TV must be turned off so you can study. Your spouse's life changes because the two of you no longer enjoy a glass of wine while analyzing the show's plot.

People in your world can support and encourage your progress towards your goal when they buy into it, or they can sabotage your efforts and detour you from your path when your goal gets in their way.

Involve Others

Always consider who might be affected by you working toward your goal. Think broadly. Make sure to consider people at work, your friends, and especially your spouse and children. It can help to write

down the names of people who may be influenced and the ways that what you plan to do might impact upon them. When you identify the possibility of a substantial impact upon someone, use this awareness to gather their support.

No one likes surprises especially when it has an impact on their life. It is a lot easier to accept change when you are involved in the decision. Even if you do not favor the ultimate decision, you will probably cooperate when your concerns have been considered. People are the most resistant when they perceive a change as being laid upon them.

When your actions have an impact on people, like your spouse or children, involve them in developing the goal itself. Don't just lay your plans on them as an accomplished fact. The more people are involved, the more they will buy-in to your goals and the steps to achieving them.

Chapter 12

Acknowledge Progress

Pay-offs and rewards are essential for maintaining the high level of motivation you need to achieve your goals. If you used the self-contracting techniques then you've built pay-offs into each step. Make sure you give yourself the pay-offs you promised yourself. You've earned them.

Self-Acknowledgement

How you think—the way you talk to yourself—about your efforts to reach your goals has an enormous impact on the quality of your journey. Depending on how you talk to yourself, you can have a joyful journey or a miserable, toil-filled time of it.

"Self-talk", as psychologists call it, is thinking—what you tell yourself about events. Self-talk is you talking to yourself in your mind. If you had critical, acknowledgement-stingy parents, chances are pretty high that you talk to yourself in the same critical, mean way they did. Berating yourself and being miserly in your self-acknowledgement turns off motivation and makes you feel small and unworthy.

Acknowledgement is powerful—and it is free! Noticing and commenting favorably on what you have done right feels good. You deserve a lot of acknowledgement for your efforts and accomplishments.

Talk to Yourself Like a Friend

Most people tend to be more critical and hard on themselves than they are on other people. We talk to ourselves in negative and depreciating ways that we would never tolerate from anyone else.

This sort of self-depreciating self-talk is not modesty; it is not being humble. It is just being down right self-abusive. People who talk negatively to themselves—and that's most of us—are usually unaware of it. The impact that negative self-talk has upon your achievements, your feelings about those achievement and about yourself is far greater than you probably realize.

Negative self-talk is a bad habit. It *is hard* to change but if you keep at it, you *will* succeed. Here's one easy technique. When you catch you criticizing and berating yourself, say "Stop!" to yourself and ask, "What would a supportive friend say about this?" Then you say it to yourself.

Chances are a good friend is going to be a lot more positive about your progress and a lot more forgiving about setbacks than you are. Talk to yourself like a good friend would. Talk to yourself in a supportive, encouraging and positive way about your efforts and progress towards your goal.

Catch Yourself Doing Something Right

Many of us tend to overlook and ignore what we do right and focus sole on what we've done less well than we wanted or on things we've failed to do. This is not helpful. It just dampens your motivation, leads to procrastination and makes you feel depressed and demoralized. It takes the joy out of the journey to your goal. Stop it!

Instead, catch yourself doing something right. Train yourself to focus on what is right or positive and good about your efforts. Even if an effort failed completely—which is unlikely—you can still acknowledge having *made* the effort. Say positive things to yourself about what you have done right and the progress that you have made. Ignore—that's right—ignore mistakes and what you haven't yet achieved.

There's a curious phenomenon that psychologists frequently observe: behavior that you pay attention to increases. If you focus on procrastination and criticize yourself for it, you'll probably procrastinate more, not less. Whereas, if you notice and acknowledge actions—however small—that get you started towards a goal, for example, it'll be easier to start in the future.

Don't expect to wipe out all negative thinking—at least not all at once. Instead, strive to reduce it. As you do, you'll see and feel the results. It'll be easier to take the needed steps to your goal and you'll feel better about your progress.

Learning to acknowledge yourself for what you've done, instead of criticizing yourself for what you haven't done, is not easy. Like any bad habit, changing it takes effort and commitment.

Keep Your Momentum Going

If you've have pushed a stick-shift car with a dead battery, you know that the hardest part is breaking the inertia and getting the car into motion. Once the car is moving it takes a lot less effort to keep it moving. The same is true of you. When you get moving, towards your goal, work at keeping a steady momentum—by taking small steps and generously acknowledging yourself for completing them.

As a general rule of thumb, give yourself more acknowledgement and pay-offs in the beginning, when you are starting, because that's when it is hardest. In the beginning you must break your inertia. Once you get moving, you can taper off a little, but don't be stingy with yourself! It is likely that from time to time your momentum will peter out and even stop. Expect this and have a plan for getting started again. As you are starting, make sure to give yourself lots of acknowledgement and many pay-offs from your Want List for starting again. Avoid criticizing yourself for having slowed and stopped. It is natural and it certainly doesn't help to whip yourself.

By being generous in your self-acknowledgement you will discover that working towards goals is a joyous journey that feels good. You don't have to wait until you reach it to feel good. Enjoy life now!

Recommended Reading

Addington, Jack E., All About Goals and How to Achieve Them, Devorss, 1977.

Adrienne, Carol, The Purpose of Your Life: Finding Your Place in the World Using Synchronicity, Intuition, and Uncommon Sense, William Morrow, 1998.

Aivanhov, Omraam M., Looking into the Invisible: Intuition, Clairvoyance, Dreams, Prosveta, 1995.

Day, Laura, Practical Intuition for Success: Let Your Interests Guide You to the Career of Your Dreams, HarperCollins, 1997.

Day, Laura, Practical Intuition: How to Harness the Power of Your Instinct and Make it Work for You, Broadway Books, 1996.

De Becker, Gavin, The Gift of Fear—and Other Survival Signals that Protects Us from Violence, Dell, 1997.

Ferguson, Gail, Cracking the Intuition Code: Understanding and Mastering Your Intuitive Power, Contemporary Books, 1999

Fisher, Milton, Intuition: How to Use it in Your Life, Wildcat, 1981.

Franquemont, Sharon, You Already Know What to Do: 10 Invitations to the Intuitive Life, Tarcher, 1999.

Garfield, Patricia, Creative Dreaming: How to Plan and Control Your Dreams, Simon & Schuster, 1974.

Gee, Judee, Intuition: Awakening Your Inner Guide, Samuel Weiser, 1999.

Gaub, Ken, Dreams, Plans, Goals: How to Have them, How to Make them, How to Reach Them, New Leaf Press, 1993.

Keen, Linda, Intuition Magic: Understanding Your Psychic Nature, Hampton Roads, 1998.

Marie, Nancy, The Beckoning Song of Your Soul: A Guidebook for Developing Your Intuition, Inner Eye, 1998.

Peirce, Penny, The Intuitive Way: A Guide to Living from Inner Wisdom, Beyond Words,1997.

Potter, Beverly A., Finding A Path With a Heart: How to Go from Burnout to Bliss, Ronin, 1994.

Potter, Beverly A., Overcoming Job Burnout: How to Renew Enthusiasm for Work, Ronin 1998.

Potter, Beverly A., Preventing Job Burnout: A Workbook, Crisp Publications, 1995.

Potter, Beverly A., The Way of the Ronin: Riding the Waves of Change at Work, Ronin, 2000.

Rosanoff, Nancy, Intuition Workbook: A Practical Guide to Discovering and Developing Your Inner Knowing, Aslan Publishing, 1991.

Sher, Barbara, I Could Do Anything If I Only Knew What It Was: How to Discover What You Really Want and How to Get It, Dell, 1994.

Sher, Barbara, Wishcraft: How to Get What You Really Want, Ballantine, 1979.

Sinetar, Marsha, To Build the Life You Want, Create the Work You Love. The Spiritual dimension of Entrepreuring. St. Martin's Press, 1995.

Stuberg, Robert. Creating Your Ultimate Destiny: The Secrets to Living an Extraordinary Life, Nightengale-Conant.

Vaughan, Alan, Doorways to Higher Consciousness, Celest Press, 1998.

Virtue, Doreen, Devine Guidance: How to Have a Dialogue with God and Your Guardian Angels, Renaissance Books, 1998.

Wieder, Marcia, Making Your Dreams Come True: A Plan for Easily Discovering and Achieving the Life You Want!, Mastermedia, 1993.

About Docpotter

Dr. Beverly Potter's work blends the philosophies of humanistic psychology, Eastern mysticism and 21st Century parapsychology with principles of behavior psychology to create an inspiring approach to handing the many challenges encountered in today's workplace.

Docpotter earned her Masters of Science in vocational rehabilitation counseling from San Francisco State and her doctorate in counseling psychology from Stanford University. She was a member of the staff development team at Stanford University for nearly twenty years.

Docpotter is a dynamic and informative speaker. Her workshops have been sponsored by numerous colleges including San Francisco State Extended Education, DeAnza and Foothill Colleges Short Courses, University of California at Berkeley Extension, as well as corporations like Hewlett-Packard, Cisco Systems, Genentech, Sun Microsystems, Becton-Dickenson and Tap Plastics; government agencies like California Disability Evaluation, Department of Energy, IRS Revenue Officers; and professional associations such as California Continuing Education of the Bar, Design Management Institute, and International Association of Personnel Women.

Docpotter has authored many books which are listed on the following pages. She os best known for her work on job burnout..

Docpotter's website is docpotter.com. It is loaded with useful information. Please visit. Docpotter would love to hear how you liked this little book on intuition and goal setting. Her email is beverly@docpotter.com.

Other Books by Docpotter

Overcoming Job Burnout

How to Renew Enthusiasm for Work
ISBN 1-57951-000-0 $14.95 302 pp.
Eight point strategy to Renew enthusiasm for work. Includes burnout test, exercises and stories.

Preventing Job Burnout

A Workbook
ISBN 1-56053-357-3 $10.95 104 pp.
An excellent partner to *Overcoming Job Burnout*. Good for training.

Audio Cassette
Beating Job Burnout
ISBN 0-914171-41-0 $9.95
How to get more job satisfaction and be more productive while avoiding job burnout.

Finding a Path with a Heart

How to Go from Burnout to Bliss
ISBN 0-914171-74- $14.95 356 pp.
A step-by-step process for leading yourself and enjoying the journey.

The Worrywart's Companion

Twenty-One Ways to Soothe Yourself & Worry Smart
ISBN 1-885171-15-3 $11.95 174 pp.
This little book offers peace of mind and a good night's sleep!

The Way of the Ronin

Riding the Waves of Change
ISBN 0-914171-26-7 $14.94 272 pp.
Shows how to multiply career options and thrive on change in the workplace.

Audio Cassette
Maverick as Master in the Workplace
The Way of the Office Warrior
ISBN 0-914171-42-9 $9.95
How to thrive on change and find fulfillment at work.

From Conflict to Cooperation

How to Mediate a Dispute
ISBN 0-914171-79-8 $14.95 194 pp.
Provides techniques for managers, supervisors, coaches, teachers, police and others who must intervene into disputes.

Drug Testing at Work
A Guide for Employers
ISBN 1-57951-007-8 $24.95 224 pp.
Describes how the tests work, legal issues employers face, setting up a drug testing program. What tests can and can't determine. Reveals how employees beat the test.

Pass the Test
An Employee Guide to Drug Testing
ISBN 1-57951-008-6 $16.95 160 pp.
Reviews employee rights, tells how to pass the test and what to do if you test positive. Written for the millions of people in corporate America who don't use drugs but still face drug testing.

Turning Around
Keys to Motivation and Productivity
ISBN 0-914171-61-5 $9.95 280 pp.
How to apply the techniques of behavior psychology to daily supervision situations in down-to-earth terms.

Healing Magic of Cannabis
ISBN 1-57591-001-9 $14.94 192 pp.
Guide to the medicinal uses of cannabis. Shows how changes in consciousness brought on by cannabis' psychoactive properties facilitate the healing process. Includes 16 medical conditions helped. How to make foods, tinctures and plasters.

Brain Boosters
Foods & Drugs that Make You Smarter
ISBN 0-914171-65-8 $16.95 256 pp.
A fascinating look at foods & drugs reported to make the mind work better. Those who want to improve mental performance will find this a valuable resource. Includes directory of life-extension sources.

Visit Docpotter's website for more useful information.

docpotter.com
beverly@docpotter.com